TWAYNE'S WORLD AUTHORS SERIES

A Survey of the World's Literature

Sylvia E. Bowman, Indiana University
GENERAL EDITOR

GERMANY

Ulrich Weisstein, Indiana University
EDITOR

Bertolt Brecht

TWAS 331

Photo by Fred Stein courtesy of Grove Press

Bertolt Brecht

Bertolt Brecht

By CLAUDE HILL

Rutgers University

TWAYNE PUBLISHERS

A DIVISION OF G. K. HALL & CO., BOSTON

Library of Congress Cataloging in Publication Data

Hill, Claude.
    Bertolt Brecht.

    (Twayne's world authors series, TWAS 331)
    Bibliography: pp. 193–99.
    1. Brecht, Bertolt, 1898–1956.
PT2603.R397Z677   832'.9'12   74–14610
ISBN 0–8057–2179–7

For

JUTTA

without whose devotion, criticism, and assistance
the completion of this book would have taken
still longer than it did.

Contents

About the Author

Claude Hill is well known to teachers and students of modern German literature and civilization. Born in Berlin in 1911, he received his Ph.D. in 1937 from the University of Jena and came to the United States a year later. Having worked as director and commentator for the Voice of America during the war, Professor Hill reentered academic life in 1946, accepting a position at Rutgers University. There he has devoted himself to developing and supervising the graduate program in German. His various activities have resulted in an honorary fellowship at the Yale Drama School, in radio productions both in New York and Cologne, in a faculty-study fellowship from the American Council of Learned Societies, in German lecture tours under the auspices of the State Department, and in faculty-study awards from Rutgers Research council. *Brecht in The Seventies,* a Brecht Symposium held at Rutgers in 1971 was organized and hosted by Dr. Hill.

Among Claude Hill's publications are *Das Drama der deutschen Neuromantik* and *The Drama of German Expressionism* (a bibliography, together with Ralph Ley). His annotated anthologies and textbooks include *Drei Nobelpreisträger, Drei zeitgenössische Erzähler, Zweihundert Jahre deutscher Kultur, Kästner für Studenten, Lesen mit Gewinn.* His articles and numerous book reviews have appeared in professional journals such as *Germanic Review, German Quarterly, Monatshefte, Modern Drama, Symposium, Books Abroad,* and also in *The New York Times, The Saturday Review, Die Zeit, Universitas,* and various German newspapers.

Preface

While there is little agreement on Bertolt Brecht, the man, the poet, the playwright, the director, the theorist of a new theater, and the advocate of Marxism, there is no doubt about his stature as one of the most famous writers of the twentieth century. His plays are being performed, by professionals as well as by laymen, in most major cities on all continents and even in the remotest corners of the earth; some of his songs and poems, often sung or recited by heart, are familiar to millions throughout the world. And yet, in America it is mainly the slogan of the "epic theater" by which Brecht is superficially and inadequately known, while only some of his plays have been professionally produced and a great deal of his work has remained untranslated, including most of the poetry. It is thus doubly difficult for the reader who has no access to the original German to form an objective picture of an author whose image has also been beclouded by cultism and political prejudice.

Of the books in English attempting a comprehensive study of Brecht, only one is relatively recent and written by an American. The very informative *Bertolt Brecht* (New York: Citadel Press, 1967) by Frederick Ewen does not quite live up to its subtitle: *His Life, His Art and His Time*, however, and mainly restricts itself to tracing the development of the playwright. While researched with full access to the Brecht Archives in East Berlin and highly commendable, the book is too detailed for the general reader and, at the same time, too brief in its treatment of the major plays. The most useful general monographs on Brecht were written in England more than a decade ago but are also available in this country: John Willett, *The Theatre of Bertolt Brecht* (New York: New Directions, third edition, 1968), and Martin Esslin, *Bertolt Brecht: The Man and His Work* (Garden City: Doubleday Anchor Books, revised edition, 1969). While Willett investigates the Brechtian theater from eight different aspects, Esslin chiefly focuses on the playwright's political development, which, he believes, constituted "a choice between two evils." In neither work is a coherent discussion of the individual plays or a general evaluation of Brecht's poetry to be found. The two Americans who most recently authored books on Brecht, Charles Lyons and John Fuegi (see Bibliography), deal with the dramatist and restrict themselves to interpretations of what they consider to be the most important plays.

This book, then, I hope, will fill an existing and often noted gap. To the best of my knowledge, it constitutes the first attempt at presenting, as completely as possible, an up-to-date, scholarly, and yet brief introduction to Brecht. Since the *World Authors Series* addresses itself to the educated general reader and not to the specialist, I have tried to express myself as simply as possible. Nevertheless, I have not refrained from taking issue with some Brecht scholars when I disagree with their conclusions, and have stated my own opinions whenever warranted. A close familiarity with Brecht's work in the original German as well as in English translation, supported by a reasonably complete knowledge of the secondary literature in both languages, and augmented by two visits to the Brecht Archives in East Berlin, including interviews with Helene Weigel and Elisabeth Hauptmann, has sustained this book which claims neither completeness nor any degree of definitiveness in evaluation. I have deliberately refrained from treating Brecht's role as an adapter of older plays, as a stage director, and as a novelist. Although it is admittedly difficult to draw the line between mere adaptation and the creation of an original drama in the case of an author whose inspiration was frequently sparked by already existing plays, it seems to me that the American reader would gain little by being informed about adaptations, most of which are not available in English. As to the director Brecht of the internationally acclaimed Berlin Ensemble, most of the pertinent literature, including his carefully prepared model books, is also unavailable. Furthermore, a detailed treatment of stagecraft would clearly seem to be beyond the scope of a series which is devoted to critical studies of major literary figures. Finally, Brecht's novels are generally considered inferior to the rest of his protean production; only one, *Der Dreigroschenroman* (The Threepenny Novel), has been translated into Eng-

Preface

lish, while most of his (far superior) short fiction exists only in German. It is for these reasons that I have concentrated on the three areas which represent Brecht's greatest achievement: his plays, his theory of the epic theater, and his poetry.

The Brecht critics and scholars to whom I feel most closely attuned are John Willett and Eric Bentley, whose refreshing and unconventional comments I had occasion to enjoy when they participated in a Brecht symposium I organized and hosted on the campus of Rutgers University in 1971. Willett's common-sensical approach and British no-nonsense insight into Brecht's affinity to Anglo-Saxon models and the English language were helpful to my chapter on poetry, and I find myself in special agreement with Bentley's "nonacademic" but sensitive insistence on stressing Brecht's charm and naïveté. Indirectly, the discussions I had with my former student and current colleague Ralph Ley have also aided me, notwithstanding some disagreement about the definition of the term "Scientific Age."

CLAUDE HILL

New Brunswick, New Jersey

Acknowledgments

Acknowledgment should be made to Hill & Wang, New York, for letting me use two excerpts from *Brecht on Theatre* (1964) in the translation of the editor John Willett: "Notes on Erwin Strittmatter's play *Katzgraben*," pp. 247–48, and "Three Cheers for Shaw," pp. 10–11. Max Knight's and Joseph Fabry's translation of "Das Lied von der Moldau" from *Schweyk in the Second World War* is from the forthcoming *Collected Plays,* Vol. 7, copyright © 1975 by Stefan Brecht, reprinted by permission of Pantheon Books, a Division of Random House, Inc. All quotations in the original German are taken from the editions by Brecht's West German publisher, Suhrkamp Verlag, Frankfurt am Main. Since American readers owe their acquaintance with Brecht's works to the various translations published by Grove Press, New York, English passages, unless specified otherwise, are taken from Grove Press editions currently in print. For a few short poems and dramatic scenes not available in English, I had to use my own translations. Each poetry quotation in Chapter 7 is followed by the name of the translator.

Chronology

1898   Eugen Berthold Brecht born in Augsburg on February 10.

1914   Poems and essays, under the name of Berthold Eugen, appear in the literary supplement of *Die Augsburger Neuesten Nachrichten,* the local newspaper.

1916   First poem signed by Bert Brecht, "Das Lied von der Eisenbahntruppe von Fort Donald" (The Song of the Fort Donald Railroad Gang) (later in *Die Hauspostille* [Manual of Piety]) appears in the same paper.

1917   Graduates from high school and enrolls at University of Munich.

1918   Attends seminar of Professor Arthur Kutscher and writes first version of *Baal* from March to June. Military service as medical orderly in an Augsburg army hospital. Writes "Legende vom toten Soldaten" (Legend of the Dead Soldier). Brief membership in Soldiers Council after the November revolution.

1919   First version of *Trommeln in der Nacht* (Drums in the Night) under the title of *Spartakus.* Beginning friendship with the novelist Lion Feuchtwanger. Brecht's first (illegitimate) son, Frank, born. Writes five one-act plays, inspired by the Munich comedian Karl Valentin, and starts reviewing plays for a socialist paper in his native town.

1922   First performance of *Trommeln in der Nacht* in Munich (September), for which he receives the Kleist Prize from the leading Berlin critic, Herbert Ihering, in November. Marries the singer Marianne Zoff, whom he met in 1919.

1923   Birth of first daughter, Hanne. *Im Dickicht der Städte* (In the Jungle of Cities) produced in Munich; first performance of *Baal* in Leipzig creates a scandal.

1924   Directs his *Leben Eduards des Zweiten von England* (Life of Edward the Second of England), written in collaboration with Lion Feuchtwanger in Munich. Finally moves to Berlin, which he had tried to "conquer" before, and becomes assistant to the producer Max Reinhardt. The actress Helene Weigel, whom he met in 1923, gives birth to Brecht's second son, Stefan.

1926 *Mann ist Mann* (A Man's a Man) opens in Darmstadt. Interest in the wheat market leads to readings in economics and first acquaintance with Marx.

1927 Attends for a while the lectures of the Marxist sociologist Fritz Sternberg. Divorce from Marianne Zoff. Brecht's first book of verse, *Die Hauspostille* (Manual of Piety) which had been privately printed under the title *Die Taschenpostille* (Pocket Manual) the year before, is published.

1928 *Die Dreigroschenoper* (The Threepenny Opera), music by Kurt Weill, opens at the Theater am Schiffbauerdamm in Berlin and becomes a sensational success.

1929 Marries Helene Weigel.

1930 Premiere of the opera *Aufstieg und Fall der Stadt Mahagonny* (The Rise and Fall of Mahagonny), music by Kurt Weill, in Leipzig. Helene Weigel gives birth to Brecht's second daughter, Barbara. First performance of *Die Massnahme* (The Measures Taken) in Berlin.

1932 *Die Mutter* (The Mother) is given the first theater production and *Die Heilige Johanna der Schlachthöfe* (Saint Joan of the Stockyards), a condensed broadcast reading in Berlin. Brecht and his circle attend lectures by the ex-communist scholar Karl Korsch and form a study group on the theme of materialistic dialectics.

1933 One day after the Reichstag fire in February, Brecht leaves Germany with his wife and son Stefan. He moves from Prague to Zürich, Lugano, Paris, and finally Denmark, where he settles on the Island of Fünen near Svendborg.

1935 Trip to Moscow for discussions about antifascist actions, plans for periodicals and theaters in German, and speeches over the radio. Brecht is officially deprived of his German citizenship by the Nazi government. Speaks at International Writers Congress in Paris and attends final rehearsals and opening of *The Mother* at the Civic Repertory Theater in New York.

1936   Attends International Writers Congress in London. First performance of *Die Rundköpfe und die Spitzköpfe* (Roundheads and Peakheads), in Danish, in Copenhagen.

1937   International Writers Congress in Paris. First performance of *Frau Carrars Gewehre* (Senora Carrar's Rifles), with Helene Weigel, in Paris.

1938   Writes first version of *Leben des Galilei* (Galileo).

1939   Leaves Denmark for Sweden and settles in Lidingö near Stockholm. Writes *Mutter Courage und ihre Kinder* (Mother Courage and Her Children) and the radio play *Das Verhör des Lukullus* (The Trial of Lucullus).

1940   After the Nazi invasion of Denmark and Norway, leaves Sweden by boat for Helsinki. Works on *Der Gute Mensch von Sezuan* (The Good Woman of Setzuan). As a house guest of the writer Hella Wuolijoki, writes *Herr Puntila und sein Knecht Matti* (Mr. Puntila and His Servant Matti). Waits for American visa.

1941   Departs for the United States via Leningrad, Moscow, Vladivostok. Arrives in Los Angeles and settles in Santa Monica near Hollywood.

1942   Works on script for Fritz Lang's film *Hangmen Also Die* and writes *Die Gesichte der Simone Machard* (The Visions of Simone Machard) together with Feuchtwanger.

1943   Writes *Schweyk im Zweiten Weltkrieg* (Schweyk in the Second World War). News reaches him that his first son, Frank, has been killed on the Russian front. Prolonged stay in New York. Actively engaged in organizing a "Council for a Democratic Germany."

1944   Writes *Der Kaukasische Kreidekreis* (The Caucasion Chalk Circle).

1945   Collaborates with Charles Laughton on the English version of *Leben des Galilei*.

1947   Premiere of *Galileo* (with Laughton) in Beverly Hills. Appearance before the House Committee on Un-American Activities on October 30. Flies to Paris the next day. Moves to Switzerland, and is commissioned to adapt and stage Sophocles' *Antigone* for the theater in the City of Chur.

1948   First production of *Herr Puntila und sein Knecht Matti*
        (Mr. Puntila and His Servant Matti) in Zürich. Meets
        Max Frisch. Works on *Kleines Organon für das Theater*
        (A Short Organum for the Theater).

1949   *Mutter Courage and ihre Kinder* (Mother Courage and
        Her Children), with Helene Weigel in the lead and guest-
        directed by Brecht, opens in East Berlin. Returns to
        Zürich, where he writes *Die Tage der Commune* (The
        Days of the Commune). Finally settles in Berlin after
        applying for Austrian citizenship. Opens his first Berlin
        Ensemble season with *Herr Puntila und sein Knecht Matti*
        on November 8.

1950   Receives Austrian passport.

1951   Awarded East German National Prize. The revised *Lukul-
        lus* script (with music by Paul Dessau) is produced by
        the State Opera under the title *Die Verurteilung des Lu-
        kullus* (The Condemnation of Lucullus).

1953   During workers' rebellion on June 17 dictates letter to
        Ulbricht (who "edits out" most of it) and to the Russian
        High Commissioner.

1954   Vice-President of East German Academy of Arts. The
        Berlin Ensemble production of *Mutter Courage und ihre
        Kinder* receives the first prize at the International Theater
        Festival in Paris. Brecht awarded the International Stalin
        Peace Prize.

1955   Plans a play on the life of Einstein. Travels to Moscow
        to receive the Stalin Peace Prize. Accompanies the Ber-
        lin Ensemble to Paris, where his production of *Der
        Kaukasische Kreidekreis* is highly applauded.

1956   Rehearsals for *Leben des Galilei* interrupted by hospi-
        talization and rest periods in his Buckow country house.
        Dies in East Berlin on August 14 and is buried in the
        old cemetery, adjacent to his apartment, near the grave
        of Hegel.

CHAPTER 1

Concerning Poor B.B.

IN an annotated volume of Goethe's autobiography there is a footnote that has often served as a devastating epithet of literary scholarship. Commenting on the poet's statement to the effect that he had once loved a certain young lady more than any other girl, the learned editor informs the reader that "Goethe was in error." The professor apparently knew it better. Generations of students have been amused by this story, which seems to confirm all that is wrong with bookishness in general and Teutonic pedantry in particular. And yet, the editor may well have been right. An octogenarian author dictating his memoirs could conceivably be mistaken about the degree of his affections in his early twenties; another writer may have valid reasons for distorting or misrepresenting certain facts of his life; a third one might simply be constitutionally unable to tell the truth; a fourth one could be prompted by an irresistible urge to mystify his public. On the whole, direct statements by an author in letters and essays are no more reliable than inferences based on the words and actions of his fictitious characters. Thomas Mann used to thank politely those interpreters who proved with stupendous erudition what had presumably been in his mind when he wrote his novels; he had not known it before. If Bertolt Brecht were still alive, it is hard to tell what would irritate him more: the legends and eulogies concocted by his idolators or the malicious insinuations of his debunkers. Chances are he would have suffered them both with the same shrug of ironic resignation and would have been pleased with the inevitable result: an increase in the sale of Brecht books and the number of Brecht productions throughout the world.

19

If caution is in order concerning the naïve equation of a writer's beliefs with those of his fictitious characters, or even with his own diaries and letters, the so-called facts of his life must be taken with an even larger grain of salt. Whether established and verified or not, they are of no relevance unless they add to the understanding of an author's work. The academic acts of horror committed upon a Milton ("His Life Records" in five volumes) and a Goethe ("Goethe and Dental Medicine") may have their place in something like the raw files of a literary FBI, but do they illuminate the celebrated victims' creative processes? It has long been an axiom of humanistic research that the deader the writer the better the results will be because it is safer to proceed after "all the facts are in." To write about Brecht today, however, is more like forecasting the election results before all the ballots have been counted. Although an overwhelming and constantly growing Brecht literature exists, reliable information about the man and his personal life is extremely scarce. We have a few reminiscences by old friends of his younger days and an occasional interview or glimpse from the last decade of his life, but there are more holes than are to be found in a Swiss cheese. The persons closest to Brecht —his late wife, the actress Helene Weigel, his children, his lifelong friend and stage designer Caspar Neher—have remained silent. His diaries—inasmuch as they exist—have not been published[1] and only a few letters from the early 1920's are known. Americans in particular who cannot read German are dependent on the few snippets Eric Bentley has released from time to time, on Martin Esslin's study, originally published in England in 1959, and on Frederic Ewen's nice but general book of 1967. In the absence of a documented and full biography, only a provisional sketch of Brecht's life can be attempted. For the purpose of this book it seems sufficient to emphasize what the reader will find reflected in the creative writings of the dramatist, poet, and theorist.

Eugen Berthold Friedrich Brecht was born on February 10, 1898, in the city of Augsburg, an hour's train ride from Munich and then part of the Kingdom of Bavaria. His parents had come from the regions of the Black Forest, the provinces of Badensia and Swabia, which prompted the young poet later to sing:

I, Bertolt Brecht, come from the black forests,
My mother carried me to town while in her womb I lay
And still the coldness of the woods lingers
And shall remain in me until my dying day.[2]

The proximity of Brecht's birthplace to Munich has led some
critics to attribute some of his pronounced character traits to
"Bavarian peasant cunning," but he spoke Swabian dialect and
wrote German with a typically Swabian tinge, and his often
observed thriftiness, frugality, sense of humor, and fondness
for dialectic reasoning place him close to a fellow-Swabian like
Hegel. Who else but a Swabian could detect humor in the
philosophy of Marx's godfather, as Brecht later claimed he did?
It should also be pointed out in this connection that the Brecht
clan came from the one region in Germany that, historically,
has been the cradle of rebellion and political freedom, something
that cannot be claimed for Bavaria, with her notorious nostalgia
for mad kings and right-wing putsches. In short, it is clearly
the Swabian heritage that was to manifest itself in Brecht. To
an American, used to a high degree of mobility and less formed
by definite regional patterns, the point may seem trivial, but I
am dealing with an author who, although he captured the
attention of the world, always remained close to his origin in
a curious way.

Father Brecht, manager of a paper factory, was a Catholic;
the mother, a Protestant; Eugen and his younger brother Walter
were brought up in the somewhat indifferent Lutheran tradition
characteristic of the middle classes in Germany. When Brecht
later took a militant antichurch stance, he only behaved in a
manner which was typical for many intellectuals who were dis-
enchanted with a church that, together with the nobility and the
military, sustained the class-ridden empire of the Kaiser. The
young boy who occasionally sneaked into the cathedral of his
father's faith did so probably more for aesthetic satisfaction than
out of spiritual yearning. On the other hand, it was Luther's
German Bible that impressed itself upon the future poet and
continued to color his literary style throughout his life. Asked
which book had had the greatest impact upon him, the freshly
acclaimed playwright replied: "Don't laugh . . . the Bible!" He
meant it. A great deal of Brecht's poetry is modeled after psalms,

hymns, and chorales and presented under the disguise of prayer
books; and the dialogues of many of the best plays are full of
biblical quotations and parodies.

Disenchantment with school life is a standard fixture in the
biography of a German writer; numerous novels, plays, and auto-
biographies abound with the sufferings of sensitive pupils under
the harsh discipline of cruel classroom tyrants.[3] If Eugen Brecht,
who gradually became Bert Brecht to his friends, did not suffer
excessively, he at least conformed to the national pattern by
remaining an indifferent pupil and narrowly missing expulsion.
In a composition on the famous Latin quotation "Dulce et de-
corum est pro patria mori" written in 1916, he challenged the
patriotism expected in the second year of World War I; only
the intercession of one understanding teacher saved him. Another incident reveals the future political tactician: having
flunked a decisive French test, the cunning boy added a few
marginal strokes on his own with a red pen and then complained
that his work had been marked wrong by mistake. The unsus-
pecting teacher excused himself, upgraded the score, and young
Brecht was promoted to the next higher class. With his customary cockiness, the newly established playwright later summed
up his school years with the following indolent remarks: "Ele-
mentary school bored me for four years. During my nine years
at the Augsburg *Realgymnasium* I did not succeed in imparting
any worthwhile education to my teachers. My sense of leisure
and independence was tirelessly fostered by them."[4] Nevertheless, young Eugen excelled in German composition and was apparently fond of Latin. Since Greek was not taught at his school,
he escaped the "tyranny of Greece over Germany"[5] so characteristic of the humanistic *Gymnasium*. The fact is important for
understanding Brecht's subsequent preference for Roman civilization with its more pragmatic and political tendencies over the
aesthetic and abstract impact of Greek culture that can be traced
throughout his literary work.

Whatever leisure accrued to the boy bored by his teachers
was spent in voracious and indiscriminate reading and was
put to use in the truly astonishing beginnings of a literary career.
Like Hugo von Hofmannsthal, whom school regulations forced
to sign early poems with the pen name of Loris, Eugen Brecht

published his first poems and book reviews as Berthold Eugen in local newspapers of his native city. The first editor was not only impressed by the intoxicating rhythms of the sixteen-year-old boy's poetry but also by his personality: a mixture of shyness and gregariousness, a burning hunger for life, a deep social awareness, and a total absence of sentimentality. It is interesting that even forty years later casual visitors recorded the same impressions of the famous playwright. The unusual precocity of the young boy, who—again like Hofmannsthal—was to write some of his finest poems at eighteen or nineteen while only a beginning university student, has not been adequately noted by most critics. It has been reported as if it were the most natural phenomenon. Brecht biographers found it, therefore, necessary to explain the choice of medicine at the University of Munich, to which he subsequently went in 1917, by pointing out his strong admiration for the dramatist Georg Büchner, who had also been a medical student. I have no doubt that already in his high-school years Brecht knew that he would become either a writer or nothing. Medicine would do as well as any other discipline to pacify for a while the bourgeois leanings of his father, who, after all, had to pay the bills; moreover, it seemed to offer the best chance for avoiding the draft—which, however, did catch up with him in 1918.

Brecht scholars trace the poet's violent antimilitarism to the traumatic experiences the young orderly underwent in an Augsburg hospital, and Marxist interpreters make a great deal of the revolutionary soldier councils in which he presumably took part. Even the levelheaded Martin Esslin quotes from an interview Brecht gave to the Russian writer Sergei Tretyakov in 1931: "If the doctor ordered me: 'Amputate a leg, Brecht!' I would answer: 'Yes, Your Excellency!' and cut off the leg...."[6] More recently published memories of an old friend of the early Augsburg days would undoubtedly justify the same footnote that I mentioned earlier in connection with Goethe's autobiography: "Here Brecht was in error." It seems that our poet spent a total of four months in uniform, assigned to cases of venereal disease, contracted by soldiers weary of the war and desirous of an early medical discharge. During part of his military service, orderly Brecht slept in his own bed at home, with the family maid occasionally answering the roll call for the "unavoidably detained" son of her employer. As to the soldiers' council, Brecht served as the elected representative of the military hospital for a few days and transmitted complaints about food and similar gripes of a trivial nature.[7] I do not mean to belittle the unpleasantness of Brecht's war experiences; I only wish to point out again that the relationship between a writer's visible and verifiable life and his work is considerably more subtle than is commonly assumed. One does not have to amputate a leg in order to be prompted to compose a bitter and vitriolic antiwar poem like "Legende vom toten Soldaten" (Legend of the Dead Soldier), the untimely demise of whose protagonist was revoked:

> Because the war was not quite done
> It made the Kaiser blue
> To think the soldier lay there dead
> Before his time came due.

Until 1921 Munich, often called an overgrown village, remained for Brecht "the big city." Partly commuting between his quaint attic room at home and the university and for a while residing in cheap furnished rooms, the medical student drifted more and more into the world of literature. He roamed café houses and taverns, where he could often be observed singing his biting songs and verses in a strangely high-pitched and hoarse voice to his own accompaniment on the guitar. He also wrote his first play, *Baal,* and then, shortly after the outbreak of the 1918 revolution, a second one, *Spartakus* (later renamed *Trommeln in der Nacht* [Drums in the Night]), "just to make money," as he cynically claimed. Lion Feuchtwanger, his elder by fourteen years and then already a successful author, was deeply impressed by the thin, unkempt, badly shaven, and emaciated young genius. He helped him, but it took several years until Brecht became prominent on a national scale; initially, only a small but devoted circle of fanatically loyal friends sustained the ego of the unpublished poet and dramatist. The ability to attract friends and collaborators, which the world-famous author was to retain until his death—and even beyond—already manifested itself in the early years of poverty, hunger, and turmoil. And although not physically attractive, the very young Brecht nevertheless succeeded with women remarkably well—possibly too much so, since already in Augsburg he found himself the father of an illegitimate son and was to marry his first wife, an Austrian singer, only a few months before the birth of his first daughter in 1922. Bohemia reigned—and not only in the realm of dreams.

It was only natural that the aspiring playwright had his eyes on Berlin, the stormy but decisive theatrical center of the nation. Although Brecht did not succeed in "cracking" the literary metropolis at his first try in 1921 and landed, instead, in a hospital sick from exhaustion and semistarvation, he came to know a surprising number of people and created sufficient attention to persuade some of the leading critics to attend the opening of *Trommeln in der Nacht* when it was finally produced a year later in Munich. Overnight, Brecht became a name to reckon with, and a short time later the avant-garde stamped its official seal of approval on the play by way of the much coveted Kleist Prize. Leipzig followed with *Baal* in 1923, and in the same year *Im Dickicht der Städte* (In the Jungle of Cities), a new play, had its premiere in Munich. A free adaptation of Marlowe's *Edward II*, undertaken in collaboration with Feuchtwanger and under the direction of Brecht himself, followed in 1924. An eyewitness recorded his impressions during rehearsals, illustrating the work habits as both playwright and director that Brecht was to maintain throughout his life: "The director B. discovered that the author's intention could not in practice be realized on the stage. So the poet B. arrived the next morning with a rewritten and changed text. As the dress rehearsal approached, B. became more and more busy, handing up whole reams of new text to the actors from the auditorium."[8] In view of the often presented charge that the older Brecht changed his plays for reasons of political expediency, it may be noted that his colleague Feuchtwanger reported as early as the 1920's that twenty or thirty revisions were nothing unusual in the texts of Brecht's plays, and that even a printed version had always to be regarded as the last but one.

When Brecht moved permanently to Berlin in 1924 in order to become a consultant and assistant director of the famous producer Max Reinhardt, he had arrived professionally if not yet financially. His plays began to be performed and read in printed form, his poems appeared in newspapers, and interviews with the young man "from the black forests" disclosed a not so "poor B.B." who sang of himself:

> I am at home on pavements. From the beginning
> Well provided with extreme unction. Sacrament
> Of newspapers. And tobacco. And likewise brandy.
> Mistrustful, lazy, yet in the end content.[9]

The real Brecht, however, was far from being lazy. He was stunningly productive and threw himself with gusto into the jungle of the big city. Berlin was then what New York was to become after World War II: the hub of the intellectual and artistic world. Not pretty, not aesthetically appealing like the *gemütliche* baroque village of Munich, but brimming with activity, terrifying, cold, chaotic, clever, corrupt, wicked, feverish, foul, electrifying, and fascinating beyond measure. The new Weimar Republic, still shaken by political turmoil, drained by an inflation of insane proportions, following a precarious path of slow consolidation, was magnanimous in the support of cultural activities. Especially the theater flourished. While the long-famous private theaters of Reinhardt continued to excel in ensemble playing and star performances of a spectacular nature, the new manager of the Prussian State Theater, Leopold Jessner, created sensations with expressionistic adaptations of the classics in a new stylized stage idiom. Foremost among the theatrical pioneers, however, was Erwin Piscator, who became the originator of what he called "epic drama," inspired by technological advances (filmstrips), Russian constructivism, and a burning desire to create a political arena similar to the *Proletkult* theater in the Soviet Union. Brecht, who observed everything and got to know everybody, worked with him and learned a great deal from him.

The conquest of Berlin was neither easy nor quick. Although the shy boy from Augsburg had become the enfant terrible of the bourgeoisie and the darling of the avant-garde by the middle of the 1920's, Feuchtwanger could state as late as 1928 in an article written for English readers: "The writer Bertolt Brecht has not succeeded in Germany so far. To be sure, his plays are performed in theaters for subscribing workers [*Volksbühnen*] and on some of the larger experimental stages, and he is the favorite topic of the literary circles."[10] Brecht's comedy *Mann ist Mann* (A Man's a Man [1926]) met with a somewhat greater popular success at its opening in Darmstadt, but did not come to Berlin until two years later. In 1927, the first collection of his poetry appeared and was instantly recognized by the knowing few. In addition to the tough ballads and tender lyrics from the Augsburg and Munich days it included cynical and mocking pieces which show the poet moving in the direction of a more or less distinct literary movement called *Neo-Factualism* (Neue Sachlichkeit). Some of these poems deal with the impact of the cold big city and with a strangely fictitious America then making itself felt from across the Atlantic. Poor B.B. could now say of himself:

> I make friends with people. And I wear
> A Derby on my head as others do

And his revealing self-portrait continued:

> I gather some fellows around me toward evening;
> We address each other as "gentlemen."
> They put their feet up on my table
> And say: things will improve. And I don't ask when.[11]

Things did improve rather rapidly indeed, if not for the poor German Republic, then at least for "poor" Brecht. His faithful collaborator Elisabeth Hauptmann directed the playwright's attention to a new London revival of John Gay's *Beggar's Opera* of 1728. The material appealed to Brecht, and he adapted and modernized it. Written in 1928 and produced in the same year, *Die Dreigroschenoper* (Threepenny Opera), with the help of Kurt Weill's jazzy music, instantly conquered the Berlin audience and subsequently most stages throughout Germany and Europe. Revivals have never stopped since, and Americans will still remember Marc Blitzstein's version as one of the longest running productions in the history of the Off-Broadway theater. Just thirty years old, Brecht had now made the big time. He had become an author of world renown.

What kind of a person was this brash young man who had caused scandal after scandal and had finally arrived at riches and fame? Was he the poet who, chosen to judge four hundred entries in a contest in 1927, refused to award a prize and, instead, praised a vulgar (and not even submitted) piece about bicycle racing? Was he the lover of Bach and Mozart who rejected Beethoven for his "battlefield music" and coined instead the term "misuk" for the type of popular tunes he liked and often composed himself? Or was he the assistant director who, according to the dramatist Carl Zuckmayer, looked "like a cross between a truck driver and a Jesuit seminarian?"[12] Or the man with a convict's closely cropped hair and a leather jacket over a silken shirt, who impressed one of the leading editors of the day as a boy masquerading in Indian costumes and at the same time looking like a schoolmaster?[13] Or was he the unfaithful husband whose refined first wife, after the future second wife, Helene Weigel, had already given birth to a new son, proclaimed that the only reason for which she might divorce Brecht was her inability to accustom him to the use of soap?[14]

The editor of the influential *Literarische Welt* in the twenties, Willy Haas, otherwise blinded by political prejudice, was probably correct when he recorded as his main impression of Brecht the invisible mask the young poet seemed to wear forever. If haircut and dress indicated both a desire to be taken for "tough" and disciplined and a member of the proletariat, there are enough poems, and utterances recorded by close friends, to reveal a vulnerable heart bursting with compassion and an anguished soul cringing with existential despair. It is very evident that the deliberately cultivated surface appearance of "a regular guy" was only assumed to hide a quivering bundle of overexposed raw nerves and a highly complex personality with more than two Faustian souls tearing "poor B.B." apart. The task of the biographer is all the more difficult, since Brecht was more than usually discreet about purely personal intentions and relations throughout his life. Strongly individualistic in matters of taste and habits, in his likes and dislikes, he had only contempt for those who bare their unimportant little egos to philistine inquiry—and certain misinterpretation. One might almost say that Brecht became more and more anti-individualistic in theory because he had plunged deeper into his own abysses and knew more about the precariousness of the individual than most. It is for this reason that he despised the naïve "O Man" exposures of the German expressionists and had felt the urge to create a truly complex counterimage to Hanns Johst's poet figure in his early play *Baal*. It is for the same reason that there are very few personal love poems in the traditional sense in Brecht's work; "one," "we," "he," "she," "they," "you," and rarely "I" are his pronouns. This is why he felt impelled to test the limits of the human personality in *Mann ist Mann*, where the hero is taken apart and rebuilt like a car and, "as you will see, he has nothing to lose by it."

It is not uncommon that a highly individualistic writer, after probing and exploring in all directions, becomes, so to speak, fed up—or bored—with his own complexities. He seeks limitations for his excesses; or, differently expressed, he feels impelled to view himself and, consequently, man in general in a broader frame of reference; he leaves the muddy and shallow brook of his ego and has the urge to be submerged in the deeper sea of humanity. Thomas Mann expressed the belief that his own turn from the artist-bourgeois conflict of his earlier work to mythological themes represents a common literary switch from the individual to the typical; Gide, Joyce, Eliot, Camus, and Sartre would seem to bear him out. The fact that many German Romantic poets converted to Catholicism may be judged in the same light. In a similar way we may view Brecht's encounter with communism, which took place around 1926 according to Elisabeth Hauptmann's records, a fact she confirmed when I asked her in 1966. Brecht was at work on a drama about the Chicago wheat market and felt the need for supplementing his inadequate background in economics. A short passage from a letter of the vacationing playwright to Miss Hauptmann—"I am kneedeep in *Das Kapital*. I've got to know all this now"—is usually accepted by most biographers as the proof of Brecht's study of Marx and his turn toward communism.

While it seems pointless to deny Brecht's subsequent close association with communism, I feel that a more subtle assess-

ment of his Marxism is needed in view of the many charges and
countercharges concerning the future founder of the Berlin Ensemble after 1949. Brecht embraced Marx in a manner somewhat similar to that in which Eliot converted to Anglican
orthodoxy. The torn, chaotic, despairing, anarchistic young artist,
at the brink of nihilism and camouflaging himself under the mask
of cynicism, needed an authoritarian philosophy to sustain himself. The theories of Marx seemed to offer a rational explanation
and a remedy for the ills and injustices of the world. The young
poet Brecht had already been attracted by the stylistic sweep
of the *Manifesto* in his Munich days and had been provoked
into rendering it in verse; now the maturing dramatist set out to
"change the world because it needed it." And in the writings of
Marx he found a philosophical basis which satisfied both his
logical mind and his ethical compassion. There is no evidence
that Brecht studied and mastered the economics of *Das Kapital*
in great depth. Fritz Sternberg, an economist and sociologist who
lectured in Berlin in the twenties and befriended the dramatist,
and who should know, if anybody does, recently confirmed my
view that the motivation for Brecht's Marxism was predomi-
nantly psychological and that his grasp of communism remained
colored by idealistic and aesthetic leanings.[15] It was the young
Marx, humanist and disciple of the beloved Hegel, who attracted
Brecht. To all of this must be added the influence of his second
wife, Helene Weigel, a determined Party adherent, whom he
married in 1929, and the fact that only the communists militantly
opposed the daily growing menace of Nazism in the Germany
of the late twenties. It is, therefore, neither startling nor does
it invalidate Brecht's philosophical acceptance of Marx when his
relationship with the Party, which he never joined, remained
tenuous to the end.

The political development and the theoretical gropings of
the playwright and stage director Brecht took place simultaneously. Growing out of comments on the opera *Aufstieg und Fall
der Stadt Mahagonny* (1929, music by Kurt Weill), there slowly
evolved the idea of the "epic theater," a term much misunder-
stood and generally inflated by admirers, often revised and
modified by its creator and, finally, altogether replaced by the
words "dialectic theater." Disgust with the commercial theater

and the desire to "educate" by way of a stage that can easily be adapted to the needs and production levels of schoolchildren and workers led Brecht to write a number of didactic plays (*Lehrstücke*) which could be and, indeed, were performed by laymen in classrooms and rented halls. The most famous and most openly communist of these short dramas was *Die Massnahme* (The Measures Taken [1930]), which may be called a genuine Marxist tragedy. *Die heilige Johanna der Schlachthöfe* (Saint Joan of the Stockyards), a long verse drama, although completed in the same year, could no longer find a stage in a Germany of increasingly shrill outbursts and intimidations from the extreme right. The last production of a Brecht play in the Weimar Republic was the dramatization of Maxim Gorky's novel *The Mother* (1932).

When Hitler came to power one year later, the author whose "Legende vom toten Soldaten" had already given him a privileged place on the Nazi liquidation list a decade earlier, had to flee for his life. "Changing countries more often than shoes," as Brecht later sang, he and his wife and their two children crossed one border after another in fifteen years of an exile that took them from Germany to Austria, Czechoslovakia, Switzerland, France, Denmark, Sweden, Finland, and, finally, to the United States, where they arrived in 1941. Instead of settling in the land of Lenin, the enemy of capitalism quickly crossed Russia by way of the trans-Siberian express and embarked for Hollywood. Editor of a literary magazine published in Moscow, the playwright Brecht preferred the drudgery of trying to turn out film scripts. Why? The answer is that the artistic climate of Stalin's socialist realism was simply not acceptable to him. Already in Berlin he had frequently expressed his low opinion of the more recent status of Russian culture, and there was nothing in the early 1930's that would have caused a change in this judgment. Those who accuse Brecht of being an opportunist should realize that, after all, America did not exactly pamper the world-famous author of *Die Dreigroschenoper* and thoroughly ignored him throughout his stay; they should rather admire a writer who safeguarded his artistic and aesthetic integrity against the dangers of political infringement and enforced sterility.

Brecht devoted the first years of his exile almost exclusively to the active fight against fascism. *Die Rundköpfe und die Spitz-köpfe* (Roundheads and Peakheads [1932–34]), begun as an adaptation of Shakespeare's *Measure for Measure* in Berlin, and became a satirical comedy about Hitler's racism; the twenty-four scenes of *Furcht und Elend des Dritten Reiches* (Terror and Misery of the Third Reich) followed (1935–38) and were published, and occasionally performed in shortened versions, of which Eric Bentley's (in seventeen scenes) has become widely known to Americans under the title *The Private Life of the Master Race*. Sympathy with the anti-Franco forces in the Spanish civil war provoked the writing of a very effective but conventional one-act play, *Frau Carrars Gewehre* (Señora Carrar's Rifles [1937]), based on Synge's *Riders to the Sea*. In addition, Brecht produced a tremendous amount of political poetry and prose, some of which was broadcast by the BBC in London and Radio Moscow or printed in leaflets and dropped by Allied airplanes. Exile, which is always a shattering experience (and even more so for a writer cut off from his native tongue), proved to be a blessing in disguise for Brecht. It freed him from too narrow and rigid a control on the part of the Party; it gave him a certain distance, widened his perspectives, and, most important of all, provided him with more time for creative purposes. Already the bustling playwright of the twenties had confided to friends that he needed to get away from the Berlin theater at least once a year in order to write; now he was forcibly separated from the beloved center of his many activities, and he could read, think, and contemplate with fresh intensity. To this we must add the natural process of maturing that any artist undergoes in his forties. The results are the so-called master plays of Brecht's exile after 1938, mostly written in the isolated countrysides of Denmark, Sweden, and Finland or on the shores of the Pacific even more distant from the war in Europe. The most important of these plays are: *Leben des Galilei* (1938–39), *Mutter Courage und ihre Kinder* (Mother Courage and Her Children [1938–39]), *Der Gute Mensch von Sezuan* (The Good Woman of Setzuan [1938–40]), *Herr Puntila und sein Knecht Matti* (Mr. Puntila and His Servant Matti [1940–41]) *Der Kaukasische Kreidekreis* (The Caucasion Chalk Circle [1944–45]).

It is curious that America, which looms so large in the early work of the younger dramatist and poet, failed to inspire or even inform Brecht once he had set foot upon her soil. Although engaged in writing and selling film scenarios (mostly without success) to Hollywood, he remained in a circle of German refugee writers and artists and apparently made no effort to get close to the cultural and spiritual life of the United States. Only two human contacts proved to be of lasting importance to him, both with former Europeans, i.e., Englishmen. He was frequently a guest in the house of Charles Chaplin, whom he admired and of whom he is reported to have said: "There are only two great directors. The other one is Chaplin." Of even greater impact was Brecht's friendship with Charles Laughton, who collaborated with him on a new English version of *Galileo* in 1945, prior to starring in the play in Los Angeles and New York (1947). The reception, however, was lukewarm; and, by and large, America ignored Brecht as much as he ignored America while he was her guest. In this connection, it is interesting and revealing that he made no serious attempt to acquire American citizenship (in contrast to most German refugees in the United States, including his friends Weill and Feuchtwanger). Brecht's heart remained in Germany and it was a foregone conclusion that he would return to Europe sooner or later—all the more so since the advent of the cold war filled him with misgivings, and he mistakenly believed that America would plunge into a new era of isolationism. His departure was preceded by an appearance before the House Committee on Un-American Activities, then investigating presumed subversion in Hollywood. Brecht relished the performance worthy of his beloved hero Schweyk (whom he had borrowed from the Czech original for a play only a few years earlier). Misleading and confusing the pitifully inept members of the committee without actually lying, the author who had been a confirmed communist for two decades was dismissed by the chairman (later convicted and sentenced to jail for fraud) with explicit thanks for his cooperation. It was, one of the observers remarked, as if a zoologist had been cross-examined by apes. Thus ended the American exile in 1947.

A great deal has been written about Brecht's return to East Berlin and his activities there as a theatrical director. Most

assessments are uncomplimentary, either accusing the playwright of opportunism or of cowardice or of double-crossing
his East German masters. The real facts, however, seem to be
rather simple and not contradictory, although the motivation
for them will have to remain conjectural for some time. The
first point that must be remembered is that Brecht arrived in
Europe as a stateless person and known to be a "leftist." Since
Berlin was at first closed to him by the U.S. Military Government, he went to Zurich. Its theater had been the major outlet
for the playwright since 1933, having produced many of his most
important plays for the first time (in his absence). There is some
evidence that he was waiting for West German offers that never
came. When the East German government, with whose policies
he was in basic agreement, offered him (or, more specifically,
his wife) the management and full resources of a theater, it was
only natural that he should accept. To paraphrase Brecht's acceptance with one of his Keuner stories: "Mr. K. preferred the
town of B. to the town of A. 'They love me,' he said, 'in the
town of A., but they were friendly to me in the town of B. They
were helpful to me in the town of A., but they needed me in the
town of B. In the town of A. they invited me to the table, but
in the town of B. they asked me into the kitchen.' "[16] Brecht was
no gourmet who would be satisfied with eating a lovely dinner
(viewing a performance); he was a cook who liked to try out
his recipes (wanted to direct). Having been starved for the
diverse ingredients of a real theater for fifteen years, the proven
and gifted director wanted and needed a workshop at last. So
he seized the opportunity when it finally presented itself.

That a man of Brecht's Swabian cunning and acquired philosophical caution would surround himself with appropriate safe-
guards was to be expected. To this we must add his low opinion
of what had been practiced as "socialist realism" in Russian art
and his aversion to all bureaucracy. There is no doubt that Brecht
took deliberate precautions, but, on the other hand, some of them
accidentally arose from the situation in 1948, and his stateless
status. His application for Austrian citizenship, for instance,
originated in his and his wife's (a native Austrian's) frustrated
desire to get to Berlin. The preliminary Austrian papers induced
the Czechoslovakian authorities and the Russian Military Gov-

ernment of the Eastern Zone of Germany to grant transit visas; thus Brecht and his wife reached Berlin from Zurich via Salzburg, Czechoslovakia, and East Germany. In 1949 Brecht toyed with the idea of reviving the Salzburg Festival by settling there and producing some of his own plays; and he actually started work on *Der Salzburger Totentanz* (Salzburg Dance of Death). When the citizenship papers finally arrived in 1950, he was well established in Berlin and did not need them any more, although they probably facilitated frequent travels abroad. Brecht simply experienced what he had already stated in 1941:

The passport is the most precious part of a human being, for it is not fabricated in the simple manner of a human being. A human being can be made everywhere, in the most frivolous manner and without intelligent reason, but a passport never. For that reason it is recognized if it is good, whereas even a very good human being may not be recognized.[17]

Another example of Brecht's presumed cunning is the fact that he gave all publication rights to the West German publisher Suhrkamp. It should, however, be borne in mind that Suhrkamp was one of Brecht's old friends and collaborators of the twenties who had steered the famous and formerly Jewish S. Fischer Verlag honorably through the dark Nazi years at the risk of incurring lasting injuries from physical mistreatment in a concentration camp. Was it not quite natural for a writer to entrust his work to the only publisher he still personally knew and whose judgment he had always respected? It should not be denied that Brecht's coup was also clever and advantageous for him, freeing his printed work from possible censorship restrictions in the East and assuring a constant flow of Western royalties at the same time. Even today, years after Brecht's and Suhrkamp's death, the fact that the rights of East Germany's most famous author are vested in a Western publishing house and that all East German books by Brecht carry the humiliating imprint "by permission of Suhrkamp Verlag in Frankfurt" is a source of great embarrassment to the authorities of East Germany. It is also apparent that there are some tensions between the regime and the heirs who control the Brecht Archives, notwithstanding the fact that the late Helene Weigel was a devoted communist.[18]

Hostile critics insist that Brecht promised the authorities some new topical plays, which he never delivered, in return for the generous subsidies his theater enjoyed. It is a fact that his last full-length play, *Die Tage der Commune* (The Days of the Commune [1948-49]), was completed in Zurich before his permanent return to Berlin. Most of his other writing comes under the heading of adaptation—although the line between adaptation and original work has always been precariously thin with him. Brecht, however, delivered. He made the Berlin Ensemble the leading theatrical enterprise of the German-speaking world, whose guest appearances set examples of unparalleled craftsmanship in the capitals of the world. On any given day, visitors from the West, after braving the vicissitudes and humiliations of a wall-crossing at Checkpoint Charlie, still cheer the sold-out performances of the tiny and curiously old-fashioned Theater am Schiffsbauerdamm. When Brecht returned to Europe, he brought with him a backlog of a dozen plays he had never seen produced. Moreover, he had become, in the meantime, the recognized theorist of a new drama, which constantly forced him to formulate, reshape, and amend what he believed was the essence of his epic theater, especially in the face of many misunderstandings. Consequently, he set out to define and redefine his style in essays and discussions and to direct performances that were intended to become models for future productions of his plays. And since we have seen that directing for Brecht always meant rewriting as well, he was fully occupied with giving final shape to what he had conceived earlier without the correctives of staging. If the young playwright of 1925 had already felt that the hectic Berlin theater did not leave him enough time for creative writing, how much more must the aging and physically ailing director of a huge and complex theatrical plant have suffered from the same burden of overextended energies. It seems really quite understandable that Brecht, excluded for fifteen years from the boards that for him "meant the world," spent the remaining years of his life consolidating and, so to speak, harvesting the fruits of his genius.

The life sketch presented here so far gives, finally, another clue to the question of why Brecht never came up with a major topical play dealing with the realities of the German Democratic Republic. He seems to have tried it once, around 1951, with a play titled *Büsching*, based on an East German Stakhanovite construction worker with the name of Hans Garbe, a project which he soon abandoned, however. As I said before, Brecht always needed a certain distance to the milieus and plots of his works; he liked to distort at will and was bothered by the confinements of naturalistic "truth." He wrote about Berlin in *Trommeln in der Nacht* before he had been there, and never once while he lived there; he created an imaginary America many times before 1941 and never once used a "real" America after he had come to the United States. He presented glimpses of contemporary Germany and Spain while sitting in a remote Danish farmhouse. The admirer of Lenin used a Russian setting only once, in his adaptation of Gorky's *Mother,* years before he got to know Russia, and never again afterwards.[19] In short, Brecht seems to have needed the distance of time or space more than almost any other modern writer. Why? Could it be that he needed a sustaining illusion unhampered by the often petty confinements and correctives of reality, an illusion he denied his plays in theory but needed for practicing his craft? It would be the ultimate irony for the only great Marxist and dialectic dramatist the world has produced so far, and it certainly explains why he never wrote that topical play he was constitutionally unable to undertake.

On June 17, 1953, workers in East Berlin and in factories in the GDR rebelled against increased production norms and pleaded for a reduction of daily quotas. Violent demonstrations occurred, and Russian tanks finally quelled the dangerously spreading unrest at the request of the East German government. Brecht is said to have been deeply upset by the affair, but his actions are still in dispute. A published communication to Ulbricht, then first secretary of the Communist Party (SED)—"I feel it necessary at this moment to write to you and express my association with the SED. Yours Bertolt Brecht"—especially aroused great indignation in West Germany. We now know that Brecht was double-crossed by Ulbricht, who published only the last sentence of a lengthy and generally critical letter. Eyewitness accounts, speeches, and poems by Brecht dating from the summer of 1953 make it unmistakably clear that he sympathized with the workers and disapproved of the leaders for what he considered misguided tactics; but he apparently felt that the hour called for a basic loyalty statement from him in terms of East and West, especially since open requests for Allied intervention could immediately be heard in the West. As recently as 1966, Günter Grass made Brecht's presumed moral failure the basis for his play *The Plebeians Rehearse the Uprising*. Although the "boss" (Brecht) is presented with sympathy, there is no historical justification for the burned-out ex-revolutionary whom Grass has re-created with all the wisdom of uncorroborated hindsight. His workers are so ridiculous as to make Brecht's hesitation to take their side an act of calculated wisdom. Legends grow fast, and as long as June 17, 1953 (at best comparable to the mutiny of the sailors in the harbor of Kiel who rebelled against inferior food and orders tantamount to suicide in November, 1918), can be falsified into a political revolution and celebrated as a national holiday with inflamed speeches by former Nazis or Nazi collaborators, Brecht will be a man of questionable character to the West Germans. To the unbiased investigator, he was a Marxist who had fashioned for himself a somewhat abstract image of a humanistic ideal, eventually to be reached, after and despite deviations, transgressions, retardations, and even regressions. There was no question to which side his basic loyalty belonged. There is also no question that a man of Brecht's intellectual sensitivity had to clash with partyline strictures and bureaucratic stupidities, no less real because the functionaries happened to be communists.

Friends have reported that the aging Brecht seemed increasingly disillusioned, and the observation is probably correct. It also appears likely that he suffered from pangs of conscience at times. Who does not? On the other hand, there is ample evidence that he fought like a lion when artistic convictions were at stake—witness his defense of the sculptor Barlach against "formalism" and the stubborn refusal to have his *Verhör des Lukullus* (Trial of Lucullus), originally written as a radio play in 1939, withdrawn rather than revised as *Die Verurteilung des Lukullus* (The Condemnation of Lucullus [1951]). Brecht did a great deal to liberalize the cultural climate of the German Democratic Republic, and yet his works were less often performed in the communist world while he was still alive than in the West. He struck many compromises, to be sure, but never in matters of basic and artistic convictions. Although the greatest export commodity of his freely chosen country, he remained irritating and exceedingly uncomfortable to his masters until his premature death on August 14, 1956—and beyond, as the before-mentioned publication arrangements for his works make clear. On the simple stone in the old Huguenot Cemetery adjacent to his house in East Berlin there is only his name—no other inscription. The most fitting epitaph for Brecht—humanist, Marxist, idealist—can be found in one of his greatest poems:

> Men's strength was little. The goal
> Lay far in the distance,
> Easy to see if for me
> Scarcely attainable.
> So the time passed away
> Which on earth was given to me.[20]

CHAPTER 2

Praise Ye the Cold, the Darkness, and Corruption!

W HEN Brecht started writing plays, the German theater was being flooded by a tidal wave of expressionistic productions. The search for a new man and a new morality, in opposition to and suppressed by the Germany of the Kaiser, rose to a feverish pitch of literary and artistic activities in every field. Numerous manifestos appeared, new periodicals were founded, provocative art exhibitions were held. The stage was opened to plays, thitherto banned, and the most diversified experimentation abounded. Dramas by Frank Wedekind, who had been entangled in endless censorship feuds before his death in 1918, were produced throughout Germany in the subsequent decade. Arthur Schnitzler's *Hands Around*, considered unstageable even by its creator, could now be performed. Georg Büchner, socially conscious iconoclastic genius of the early nineteenth century, was rediscovered. Georg Kaiser, whose *Citizens of Calais* had already exuded the new spirit before the war, now occupied the center of the German theater and became the most widely produced playwright of the young Republic. "Where is the New Man?" cried the billionaire's son in Kaiser's *Gas I* (1918). "I shall give birth to Him," answered his daughter, thus stating the credo of the new movement.

Most of the leading expressionists had spent their formative years in opposition to the Establishment during the first decade of the century; that is to say, their convictions were grounded in an unshakable idealism that no odds could shatter. Man was basically good, and if the ills of modern society (chauvinism, greed, injustice, class consciousness, mechanization) could be cured, man would respond to the challenges of his potential nature. Utopia seemed around the corner, so to speak. Utopia, however, remained as distant after 1918 as it had been before. Imperial Germany collapsed, the Kaiser fled, revolution and

40

civil war followed, democracy was established—but what had
basically changed? Was militarism dead? Had a new social spirit
arisen? Was justice being fairly administered? Had poverty
been extinguished? What about inflation, prostitution, slums,
anti-semitism, political murder, unemployment, economic depression, crime, debauchery, anxiety, and alienation? The
younger artists, who had been dragged to war from the benches
of high schools and had come home bitter and broken, no
longer believed in anything. Too young to be fortified with a
sustaining philosophy of their own and too old to start from
scratch, they became confused, disillusioned, and, finally, cynical.
To them, the rhetoric of the older expressionists appeared
shallow, their faith naïve, and their slogans spent. There seemed
to be only one thing one could be sure of: being alive. Enjoy
today because you don't know what tomorrow will bring!

Brecht was sixteen when the war broke out, twenty when he
was drafted as a medical orderly and witnessed the revolution
in Munich, and only slightly older when he set out to conquer
the jungle of the terrifying city of Berlin. He thus belonged to
that "generation between chairs" to which we owe novels like
Hemingway's *A Farewell to Arms,* Remarque's *All Quiet on the
Western Front,* and poetry like Eliot's *Wasteland* or Erich
Kästner's *Hausapotheke.* The decisive experiences of the young
Brecht were despair and cynicism caused by the chaotic conditions in postwar Germany. To which we must add an unusually
strong sensuality, a peculiar fixation on the rot and decay of or-
ganic life, and an excessive individualism bordering on anarchy.
As to early literary influences, the wild outsiders and outcasts of
society, such as Villon, Rimbaud, and Verlaine, fascinated
Brecht; Kipling's ballads set the tone for an imaginary Anglo-
Saxon world of tough and "manly" heroes which the young
poet from Augsburg was to re-create over and again; finally
there was Wedekind, whose mocking *chansons* and disturbing
plays had shocked the German bourgeois and delighted the
young rebel, who had seen the great man perform in Munich.

I Baal

What Professor George Pierce Baker's dramatic workshop at
Harvard ("Playwriting 47") was for O'Neill, Arthur Kutscher's

seminar on the theater at the University of Munich was for Brecht—with one decisive difference. The two Germans did not like each other, and there is no evidence that the brilliant young student ever learned anything from the rather limited teacher whose only claim to fame was a personal friendship with Wedekind. However, the seminar provided the aspiring dramatist with a forum for discussion and, accidentally, provoked the writing of his first play. In the spring of 1918, the young student read a paper on the expressionistic writer Hanns Johst (later the leading Nazi playwright), whose drama *The Lonely One* had just opened in Munich. To the increasing rage of Professor Kutscher, Brecht tore Johst's opus apart and arrogantly vowed that he would write a better "counterplay" on the same theme and with the title *Baal*. At the end of July, he submitted the completed manuscript to the still indignant professor.

The Lonely One is a historically more or less accurate dramatization of the disintegration and death of Dietrich Christian Grabbe, one of the "wild" German dramatists of the early nineteenth century. While less esoteric and more realistic than many other expressionistic dramas, Johst's nine scenes are nevertheless replete with overblown idealistic rhetoric and even call for the music of Beethoven for increased effect. The play essentially conforms to the sentimental clichés of the philistine about a so-called genius destroyed by the conventions of society. Brecht's counterhero is a modern vagabond, a rake, and finally a murderer, a fat clump of expanding tissue, an unwashed, loud, lewd mountain of a man with titanic appetites— and yet also a tender poet at times, a childlike prankster, and always a human being of unbending honesty. We see him wooed by publishers whom he insults and female admirers whom he seduces or even rapes or drives to suicide. After he has become tired of women, he indulges in a homosexual relationship with his closest friend, the composer Eckart, whom he kills in a bout of jealousy. Hunted by the police, mortally exhausted and abandoned by everybody, he finally dies alone in a hut in the woods "like a rat." The name of Brecht's poet gives a clue to his mood and intentions: Baal is the ancient Semitic god whose worship was characterized by fertility rites and human sacrifice and who gradually became a synonym for evil in the Judaeo-

Christian tradition. Baal is also Brecht, and more specifically, the young skinny Bert of Augsburg's meadows and taverns who projected the fulfillment of his wishes onto a fat, lusty stage hero.[1]

Needled by Johst's solemn treatment of the doom of a poet, Brecht referred to his play as "comedy" while he was working on it and injected elements of parody, especially into those scenes in which the poet Baal confronted an audience of admirers and professionals from the literary world on the stage. However, the prevailing mood throughout most of the play is a hymnic evocation of nature at its wildest, rawest, and most violent. While the work is dramatically weak (too many short scenes, no three-dimensional characters besides Baal, no development), it is the language that distinguishes it from thematically similar outbursts of other young German writers. Although many influences can be traced (the friendship of Verlaine and Rimbaud reflecting the relationship between Baal and Eckart, the dramatic style of Büchner's *Woyzeck,* the dialogue technique of Wedekind, the word cocktails of Rimbaud), Brecht wove them into a unique fabric of his own creation which fused the tender with the harsh, the delicate with the brutal, the mocking with the hymnic, the refined with the coarse, the modern with the classical. The nineteen-year-old writer found here the idiom which was to remain essentially the same throughout his work and which proved to be as inimitably Brechtian as it was unsuccessfully imitated by others.

In view of many legends and mystifications surrounding Brecht, a few observations concerning the writing of his first play may be helpful, especially to those readers who must rely on materials published in English. The often repeated story (even by Martin Esslin) that Brecht wrote *Baal* in four days in order to win a wager with a friend is not true. We may now assume that he worked on the first draft for at least six weeks (1918), that he reshuffled and revised the scenes in 1919, and that he totally rewrote and condensed the play in 1926 for a Berlin production under his own direction, in keeping with the theories of his newly developed epic theater: there are only twelve scenes left now; Baal has become an auto mechanic; and the tone has cooled to the temperature of Neue Sachlichkeit

(New Factualism). The "official" version known today and translated into English is essentially the third one (twenty-four scenes) of 1922. Even if we consider the first two similar drafts as one, we have three distinctly different versions of the same play. It may be argued that the relatively unknown one of 1919 (twenty-eight scenes) is perhaps the richest and most poetic. The history of the first play points up one of the difficulties confronting not only the Brecht scholar but also the uninformed lover of his work. In regard to *Baal* it is evident that the young author gradually moved away from Johst's model and also eliminated certain autobiographical elements. Baal's mother has disappeared in the first printed edition of 1922 (Brecht's mother, to whom he was very close, had died in 1920), and so has the scene showing Baal as a reviewer, which is reminiscent of the days when the young student had contributed to newspapers in Augsburg. This is characteristic of Brecht: throughout his life, he was careful to reveal as little as possible about himself in his plays.

On the occasion of the 1926 production in Berlin mentioned earlier, Brecht published an article on "The Model for Baal," in which he named a mysterious Josef K., a skilled mechanic who never worked, lived the life of a vagabond, rake, and murderer, and presumably died in the Black Forest. Scholars have made a great deal of this "revelation." They either attribute special affrontery to Brecht for juxtaposing an uneducated mechanic to Johst's literary hero, or they take it as proof of Brecht's early social concern, as for instance the Marxist scholar Ernst Schumacher has done. In view of the fourth version, however, in which Baal has indeed become a mechanic, it seems obvious to me that Brecht simply indulged in one of his mystifications, which he liked so much. The style of the article (probably written by his collaborator E. Hauptmann) clearly indicates mockery. There was no living model for Baal. There were only certain ingredients in Brecht's own experience that triggered the fictionalized self-portrait of the chaotic and amoral nihilist of 1918.[2] It was not until five years later, after Brecht's second play had been received with wide acclaim, that a producer dared to put *Baal* on a stage. Scandal and protest greeted the Leipzig opening as well as the subsequent performances in Munich and Berlin.

While one critic referred to the play as "a mud-bath" and the audiences were either shocked by the many obscenities or disappointed by the total absence of a dramatic plot, few could escape the impression that they had heard a powerful new voice of the younger generation. Even a poet as remote from Brecht as Hugo von Hofmannsthal, the elegant, aristocratic, and gentle representative of Old Austria, welcomed the Vienna production of *Baal* in 1926 with a prologue from his own pen in which he stated: "A play like this is entirely of one piece.... What you have here is word and gesture as one and the same thing. An inner life bursting forth and creating a new world, filling it with its own vital force."[3]

II Trommeln in der Nacht
(Drums in the Night)

Although Brecht's rejection of expressionism had occurred as early as 1917 (according to the published memoirs of an old friend),[4] it was inevitable that the powerful sweep of the new movement could still be felt in the first dramatic works of the nineteen-year-old novice playwright. No beginning German writer of his generation could remain immune to the radical demand for a new image of man and to the intoxicating ecstasy of a new style. If Baal was not Kaiser's "New Man," he was certainly the ne plus ultra projection of a new amoral vitality transcending the bounds of traditional individualism. Moreover, the stylistic influences of Büchner and Wedekind, grandfather and godfather of expressionism, are also visible and audible in *Baal,* as has already been pointed out. To a still greater degree, this is true of Brecht's second play, which he wrote in 1919, and which made him famous. It deals with the theme of the returning soldier, frequently treated by expressionists; and it is for this reason that the early Brecht has often been called expressionistic.

The novelist Lion Feuchtwanger, who was also a successful playwright before his American exile, and who was acting as literary adviser to a Munich theater in 1919, suggested the title *Trommeln in der Nacht* for the script the young emaciated genius had submitted to him as *Spartakus.* It was called a

comedy, a label only fitting if comedy simply means that the
hero does not die at the end. Otherwise, with the possible
exception of the parodistic opening scene, it must be called
one of the unfunniest comedies even according to German
standards. Andreas Kragler, belatedly released from an African
prison camp and believed to be dead, returns to postwar
Berlin, in the midst of counterrevolutionary struggles, and finds
his fiancée Anna engaged to, and pregnant by, another man,
and joins his fellow workers. But having a change of heart
when Anna runs after him, he betrays "his class" by abandoning
the revolution, and goes home to the "big, wide bed." The
young Brecht, who had obviously based the play on personal
observations during the stormy days of Bavaria's short-lived
regime of the radical, independent socialist leader Dr. Kurt
Eisner, claimed that he had written it in three days in order
to make money. There is no reason to doubt him, because
Baal was still unpublished and unproduced, and the feverishly
ambitious and creative medical student was starving for a
breakthrough. He had to wait another three years. *Trommeln in
der Nacht* was first performed in 1922 in Munich, the production
was widely acclaimed, and followed by some forty other ones
elsewhere in Germany. It won the highly prestigious Kleist
Prize for the young author who, at the age of twenty-four, had
now become the enfant terrible of the German theater.

When Brecht prefaced an edition of his collected plays in
1954, he was embarrassed by the obvious cynicism and egotism
of his early hero, who could not even remotely be reconciled
with a Marxist attitude. I was all the more surprised when his
widow, the militantly communistic Helene Weigel, told me, as
late as 1966, that she had always had a special affection for
this play, which she considered one of her husband's best.
Aesthetically, it is indeed a well-made play, almost traditional
in its five-act structure and Aristotelian compression of time. It
has, in contrast to *Baal*, a number of sharply drawn, acidly
etched minor characters (Anna's parents and her fiancé) that
call to mind the devastating family satires of Brecht's painter
friend George Grosz. The mature Marxist playwright of 1954
was undoubtedly correct when he cited as excuses for his
youthful attitude both his contempt for the optimistic "O Man"

outbursts of the expressionists and his own uninformed, romanticizing view of the revolution. At the same time, Miss Weigel seems to have put her finger on the issue that still gives validity to the play: the early betrayal of the 1918 revolution by the "moderate" socialists and the refusal of most German veterans to join. Surrounded by greedy, war-profiteering scums of the petite bourgeoisie, Andreas opts for personal happiness. Young Brecht, as yet unenlightened by Marxist doctrines, had been in the midst of revolution and counterrevolution and had, undoubtedly, been deeply disappointed by what happened. He saw primarily the bloody turmoil around him, and his Baalian instinct fed on the anarchy and chaos of the surface events. What gives the play its literary distinction is, as in *Baal*, the linguistic idiom, which, in its incomparable mixture of stark realism, ironic allusions, and earthy imagery, reveals a new twentieth-century man, totally devoid of sentimentalism and self-pity and eluding traditional psychology.

III Im Dickicht der Städte
(In the Jungle of Cities)

Brecht's third play is his most obscure and baffling one. It is interesting also in terms of the author's uncanny ability to camouflage his intentions, and occupies an important position in the history of twentieth-century drama. Unknown to the English-speaking world until 1961, when Bentley translated and Off-Broadway produced it, the play was immediately recognized as a powerful statement of the Theater of the Absurd some three decades before Beckett, Ionesco, and Pinter. Nevertheless, no penetrating study or convincing interpretation has been attempted so far; and, as is to be expected, Brecht's own introduction of 1954 is of little help. Some of his recollections are at variance with those of his closest friends of the early 1920's, and his inclination to project pre-Marxist notions of capitalism before he admittedly read Marx must be dismissed as wishful thinking in retrospect. The following remarks must be taken as attempts at a tentative interpretation subject to verification or rebuttal on the basis of hitherto unpublished material.

George Garga, a clerk in a Chicago lending library, is

confronted by Shlink, a Malayan lumber dealer, who wants to
buy his opinion about a book. Garga refuses. We soon learn that
this is only the pretext for a fundamental challenge: Garga's
whole identity is at stake, and from the opening scene a
baffling fight to the finish between the two men ensues. Each
one throws all of his resources into the duel: the fifty-one-year-old
Asiatic his business, his underworld connections, and his own
physical labor; and the young bachelor his parents, his sister,
girl friend, and, most precious of all, his own personality, which
is being transformed from honest dreaminess to realistic cunning.
Toward the end, they realize that human isolation is so great
that not even a death struggle like theirs can establish contact.
Before a lynching mob set on his trail by Garga reaches him,
Shlink poisons himself, while Garga, alone and hardened, sells
his possessions, including all his human contacts, abandons his
romantic dream of a "natural" life in Tahiti, and goes off to
New York. His last words are: "To be alone is a good thing.
The chaos is used up now. It was the best time."

Arnolt Bronnen, a minor German playwright and, in those
days, a close friend of Brecht, witnessed the writing of the
play and was baffled by it. He reports that when he asked
Brecht about the meaning he received the laconic answer:
"The last lines."[5] He also tells us that he easily detected Bertolt
behind Garga, and that Brecht did not deny this fact. Shlink, on
the other hand, seems to be a composite of whoever was very
intimate with the young poet at the time and was threatening
his independence as well as penetrating the carefully erected
façade of seeming toughness: possibly Bronnen himself and
(during subsequent revisions) probably Feuchtwanger, whose
features were curiously Oriental and whose diction Bronnen
recognized in Shlink's lines. There were others, of course, and
there also are readily admitted literary sources for the play:
Garga frequently recites from the German translation of Rimbaud's *A Season in Hell,* and the influence of the novel *The
Wheel,* by the Danish author J. V. Jensen, is even stronger
than Brecht hinted in the preface of 1954. It is also possible
that a silly melodrama the young Augsburg poet saw twice in
1919, because he liked it so much, aroused his scenic imagination; the play, presumably translated from the English, ran

under the title *Mr. Wu or the Revenge of the Chinaman.*[6] I am inclined to add to these sources the (perhaps unconscious) influence of Kafka, whose first publications had appeared in a series of avant-garde volumes we know Brecht was in the habit of reading. One may note the similarity in the letter combination constituting the name of Kafka's hero Samsa, who was transformed into a life-size beetle, with Garga, and compare the family relationships of both men, who are bachelors burdened with the care of a sister and a loving mother, and a somewhat parasitic father. Although my conjecture has not been supported by any witness who might be in a position to know, it seems to me that Brecht's invention of Josef K. for the model of Baal, written one year after the first publication of *The Trial* (whose hero is also called Josef K. in the same modern German spelling of the name), makes the influence of Kafka likely.[7]

Brecht wrote *Im Dickicht der Städte* during the winter and early spring of 1921–22, partly in Augsburg and mostly in Berlin while engaged in "conquering the jungle of the big city." The attempt failed, as we have seen, just as his Garga had to leave Chicago. Revisions followed in Munich, where the first performance finally took place in May, 1923. The baffled audience got increasingly angry during the seemingly less and less coherent happenings on the stage, the usual scandal erupted, and the play was withdrawn, after a few days. The reaction in Berlin turned out to be the same, and it was not until some forty years later that the significance of Brecht's writing became evident to an audience in New York, a jungle even bigger and thicker than Berlin. E. Bentley claims that the German connotation of the original title "Dickicht" is more properly conveyed by the word "swamp," but it should be pointed out that Brecht frequently used the word "jungle" as a synonym for Berlin (or any big city). In other words, one of the themes of his play is alienation and lack of communication in the increasingly urbanized society of our time, the great symbols of which are places like Berlin, Chicago, and New York. It is the swan song of the young man from the country who still has romantic notions (Tahiti) and a certain naïve integrity at the beginning, who actually loves the chaos from which he suffers ("it was the best time"), and who gradually stiffens into a new toughness he half regrets and half welcomes. He enjoys his vitality ("the younger man wins"), and he also learns to fend entirely for himself ("to be alone is a good thing"). Most important of all: he has, or he thinks he has, overcome the chaos in himself ("the chaos is used up now"), and is now ready to conquer life.

If urbanization and its depersonalizing effect on modern man is one of the themes of the play, its underlying tone is existential despair, despite the surface toughness of the dialogue. Loneliness is unbearable, and Shlink, after a lifetime of thick-skinned isolation from any human relationship, seeks personal contact, even if only by way of a meaningful struggle, as it were. He speaks to Garga of "our metaphysical fight," but cannot reach him. In the tenth scene, he comes to realize: "The endless isolation of man makes even enmity an unattainable goal. Even with animals it is impossible to come to an understanding." After Garga confirms this gloomy plight of man and adds that speech, too, is of little help, Shlink continues: "I have watched animals. Love—warmth from bodily proximity—is our only grace in all the darkness. But the union of the organs is the only union, and it can never bridge the gap of speech." We now understand why Baal is finally driven to a homosexual relationship with his friend Eckart; and we find here the explanation of why Shlink, whose concern was spiritual, also had to love Garga in a physical sense. Furthermore, the passage throws some light on the role of women in the play. Each man uses them in order to reach the other where it hurts, and that means in a fight. In a death struggle, the breaking point would be reached if one of the protagonists were to give up because he could not take "it" (i.e., humiliation and prostitution of his beloved) any longer. Brecht also plays with the time-honored notion, advanced by many psychologists and writers, that the female is instinctively closer to truth than the more cerebral male. In this connection I am again reminded of Kafka, whose women always serve the function of sexual objects through which the hero may reach the desired goal (the lawyer's secretary in *The Trial*, Frieda in *The Castle*). Whether influence or plain coincidence, *Im Dickicht der Städte* shows Brecht engaged in the kind of radical probing and questioning of the metaphysical nature of man that has come to be identified as the main concern of Existentialism.

In the preface of 1954, Brecht obliquely hinted that he may have exaggerated the formal aspects of his youthful play, and added: "Both earlier and later I worked in a different way and on different principles, and the plays were simpler and more materialistic. . . ."[8] This is a useful reminder that no appraisal of a literary work should end with a mere unraveling of its meaning. While the *what* reveals the intentions of a writer, it is the *how* that determines his stature. We have already seen that the distinction of Brecht's first two plays chiefly rests on a new linguistic idiom that disregards traditional psychology and cuts through the layers of conventional speech. We may now direct our attention to the peculiar structure of Brecht's third play, hoping to explain the seemingly zigzag course of events and some of the baffling episodes. The clue comes from the author himself, who tells the audience: "You are going to observe the inexplicable wrestling match between two men. . . . Do not rack your brains over the motives for this fight but note the human stakes, judge without prejudice the style of each contestant, and direct your interest to the finish." In other words, sport, which was then to the young what rock-and-roll is to youth today, intrigued Brecht in the 1920's and provided the structure for what he intended to be a truly modern play. We know that he later befriended the leading German boxing champion; but it does not matter whether we think of wrestling, fencing, or tennis. What matters is sport in the form of a contest to which each of the participants brings all the strength he has. We may then view the eleven scenes of the play as ten rounds plus an epilogue. At first, Shlink has the upper hand; the various episodes correspond to the technical points (some of which are fouls) scored by the adversaries, and in the end the younger and, therefore, stronger Garga wins. As in sports, there is no reason for the fight other than the competitive spirit of the contestants, and it would be useless "to rack our brains over the motives."

Since Brecht saw in the newly discovered sport of boxing "one of the great mythical diversions of the giant cities on the

other side of the herring pond,"[9] America appealingly lurked
behind the horizon of his wild imagination. At the same time,
this newly felt America seemed a proper setting for all that was
characteristic of the vision of a new man: tough, strong, young,
unsentimental, sober, realistic. Brecht's mentor-friend Feuchtwanger similarly featured American backgrounds, as did many
other German writers (Kafka, too, had left an unfinished novel
called *Amerika*), and the so-called literary movement of Neo-
Factualism in the mid-twenties was tinted with a strange picture
of a fictitious German America, which easily lent itself to grotesque distortion, partly involuntary and partly deliberate. Brecht
could not care less whether it was possible to sail from "the
piers" of Chicago to Tahiti or whether sexual intercourse between a white prostitute and a Malay merchant "born in Yoko-
hama" would provoke a lynching expedition in the "chinatown"
of the city. The fact that he stuck to these inaccuracies through
the revisions of the play shows both a contempt for detail he
considered irrelevant to his purpose, and a deliberate use of the
grotesque. The effect of the latter is enhanced by a technique
of slapstick comedy, probably inspired by Chaplin and, even
more so, by the Munich comedian Karl Valentin. It chiefly consists in taking things literally that are normally not taken at
their face value, and in stubbornly pursuing a thought to its
very end. It leads to a kind of primitive realistic symbolism, such
as the equation of physical nakedness with spiritual loneliness:
Garga's acceptance of the duel is underscored by his "losing his
shirt," which he literally does on the stage, and the act of
stripping corresponds to a kind of existential peeling of a man's
protecting warm hide. Shlink's thicker skin symbolizes both the
toughness needed to succeed in this world and the correspond-
ingly greater alienation of his spiritual nature, while Garga's
change of clothes indicates the transformation of his personality.
The devices used by Brecht are the same that were to be employed by Beckett and Ionesco and, to a lesser degree, by
Dürrenmatt and Pinter some thirty years later. *Im Dickicht der
Städte* is thus indeed one of the first plays of the Theater of
the Absurd.

IV   Mann ist Mann
(A Man's a Man)

While his next play, an adaptation of Marlowe's *Edward the Second* (together with Feuchtwanger), still pursues the theme of homosexuality as the only possible bond between men in a world of icy loneliness, Brecht's exploration of Berlin, together with his increasingly hectic involvement in the intellectual struggle of the times, brought about a shift from the chaotic and still romantic outsider to a less individualistic and more ordinary hero representing the new urban, mechanized, capitalistic age. Philosophically, the transition corresponds to an abandonment of pessimism and the acceptance of a cautious optimism, or, at least, a cynical approval of what seems inevitable. Aesthetically, Brecht's development indicates a shift from tragedy to comedy. The result was his fifth play, *Mann ist Mann,* chiefly written in Berlin between 1924 and 1926. Its theme is the transformation of the good-natured Irish porter Galy Gay into a bloodthirsty soldier of the British colonial army stationed in India. Before the decisive scene a character steps in from behind the curtain and says:

> A Man's a Man is Mister Bertolt Brecht's contention.
> However, that's something anyone might mention.
> Mister Brecht appends this item to the bill:
> You can do with a human being what you will.
> Take him apart like a car, rebuild him bit by bit—
> As you will see, he has nothing to lose by it.

And he ends with the lines:

> And he hopes you won't miss the moral of Galy Gay's case:
> That this world is a dangerous place.

Mann ist Mann is Brecht's first parable play and also the first one in which he deliberately employed some of the new technical devices of the epic theater which he was exploring in those years. It is, however, wrong to speak of an "abrupt transition," as Eric Bentley has done. Nor is it justified to see in the broad farce a youthful premonition of Marx's notion of the collective, as Brecht himself did in his preface of 1954, or a solemn expression of immature communism not yet enlightened by a knowledge of the dialectic process, as Marxist critics have done. A close investigation of the circumstances surrounding the writing and staging of the play reveals as its hero a somewhat cynical Garga, who, after surviving a death struggle (*Im Dickicht der Städte*), is now sufficiently hardened and liberated from his former "chaos," that he may successfully adjust to the vicissitudes of life, as Galy Gay does. We now know that large portions of the comedy were written as early as 1921 in Munich (title: *Der grüne Garraga* [The Green Garraga]), and that its author was then inspired by an odd deterministic but totally non-Marxist philosophy of life. When he took up the fragment a few years later in Berlin, Brecht was groping toward a new function of the theater, inspired by sport and Neo-Factualism and opposed to a personality concept which seemed to him anachronistic in its excessive individualism, as well as sentimental and pompous. What he observed in Berlin undoubtedly helped, and a new awareness of social implications should not be denied (working with Erwin Piscator made this almost inevitable), but his overriding notion then was that the theater should provide fun. Audiences ought to get the same fare and react in the same fashion as spectators of sports events do. We may, therefore, be justified in regarding *Mann ist Mann* primarily as a spoof, a theatrical joke extending over two hours, full of silly, crude, and improbable happenings, obviously inspired by Kipling, the silent movies, the tricky logic of his favorite comedian, Valentin, and the style of Luigi Pirandello.

It is interesting that Brecht cut out the last two scenes of the play for a Berlin production in 1931—that is, after he had fully embraced Marxism. Why did he do so? In the old version Galy Gay, who had been transformed into a soldier through blackmail, temptation, and fear, had been allowed to run rampant at the end. He had become a killer, a "human fighting machine," eager to outdo his comrades and driven by an uncontrollable desire for blood. The collective, i.e., the army, obviously did not demand this behavior, which also stands in contradiction to the tenets of orthodox Marxism. So the newly converted Brecht of 1931 ended the play by having Gay become a soldier before the

battle begins. It speaks for the artistic integrity of the mature
playwright that he restored the two scenes for the edition of his
collected works. The full text of the finally approved version has
Gay say before the attack at the end (not included in Bentley's
English translation): "Already I can feel the desire to sink my
teeth into the neck of the enemy, the arch impulse, to slaughter
the breadwinner of the families, and to carry out the order of the
conquerors." These lines reveal a rather dim view of humanity,
such as was still characteristic of the young Brecht, even after
he had renounced the explicit glorification of a Baal and had
turned to man's plight as a social being in *Mann ist Mann.* However, one should not misjudge the obvious intention and general
tone of this farce, which is primarily a satire and playful variation on the theme of personality in the light of Neo-Factualism,
Dadaism, Behaviorism, some dimly perceived sociological notions, and last but not least, of Einstein's theory of relativity, as
the following lines immediately preceding Gay's transformation
(not in Bentley's translation) indicate:

What does Copernicus say? What is turning? The earth is turning.
The earth, ergo: man. According to Copernicus. Which means that
man is not in the center. Now look at him. This one here is supposed
to be in the center? He is historical. Man is nothing. Modern science
has proved that everything is relative. What does this mean? The
table, the bench, the water, the shoehorn, everything relative. You,
Widow Begbick, I . . . relative. Look me in the eyes, Widow Begbick,
a historical moment. Man is in the center, but only relatively.[10]

V Die Dreigroschenoper
(The Threepenny Opera)

One of the many ironies surrounding Brecht's career and
reputation is the fact that he owes his greatest popular success
to a work that, in many respects, may be called his least original one. Even today, after thousands of performances and
revivals throughout the world, it is impossible to determine
whether the popularity of *Die Dreigroschenoper* is due to Brecht's
brilliant adaptation, to the durability of John Gay's model of
1728, or perhaps to Kurt Weill's racy music—to which we could
add the shock appeal of Villon's ballads, incorporated by Brecht.

And while, as we have seen, almost every one of his plays had a long incubation period and underwent many revisions, *Die Dreigroschenoper*, six scenes of which had been written "with his left hand," so to speak, while he was engaged in another major project, was hastily completed in a few weeks in 1928 and produced in the same year, mainly because a young Berlin impresario needed an opening vehicle for his first season. Even during the dress rehearsal there was still universal gloom, and the participants braced themselves for the biggest flop in history. But the production turned out to be the greatest sensation of the German theater in the twenties. It remained Brecht's only popular success until some thirty years later, and conquered practically all of Europe. Only in the United States did the first showing (in 1933) fail to provoke a comparable response, mainly as a result of an inferior production; but a 1954 revival in Marc Blitzstein's version at the Theater De Lys secured one of the longest runs in the history of Off-Broadway theater.

Almost everybody knows the story of the robber Macheath, mainly through Weill's song of "Mack the Knife" and other tunes and juke box recordings; and there is no need for summarizing the plot. It is, however, revealing to compare the modern German adaptation with its English model. Gay wrote a topical musical in which he satirized the upper classes and the high society of his time. The audience easily recognized, for instance, in the character Lockit of *The Beggar's Opera* the Prime Minister Sir Robert Walpole. The general point of view prevailing in the play seemed to be the similarity between the ruling aristocrats and the rogues of eighteenth-century England. Brecht, who, in the meantime, had read Marx, transposed the setting to late Victorian London. Lockit became the police chief Tiger Brown and, thus, a symbol of the corrupt middle class, and Mr. Peachum now organized the beggars of London into a tightly disciplined business enterprise, in keeping with the Marxist notion of the bourgeoisie taking over the role of the aristocracy. Brecht's satire, however, was not directed at an easily recognizable target. Nor did a Victorian London provide a significant frame of reference to the Germans of 1928. Although Macheath was intended to be a reprehensible gangster who simply adapts the standard practices of business under capitalism to his own immoral way of life, he remains too much a charming, even romantic, he-man, sex symbol, and villain. After all, it is he, the gangster, who has the only lines that may be called revolutionary: his call for beating up policemen toward the end of the play. The operatic fairy-tale "happy" ending finally underlines the ambiguous character of any hidden social message. As a result, everybody could and did enjoy the whorehouse atmosphere on the stage, which seemed to be a small-scale replica of the larger bordello that Berlin was in the twenties. Few spectators felt that Brecht was waving his raised index finger at them. The play is opaque and amoral because its author, despite some glimpses of communist doctrine and a general sympathy for the downtrodden and exploited, was still in love with clever manipulators and Kipling's strong men, and obviously cynical about the possibilities of true social reform.

It is not surprising that Marxist critics, while appreciative of the author's sympathy with the poor, severely complained about the play's lack of social concreteness. On the other hand, most bourgeois audiences were convinced—and still are—that they had witnessed a genuine communist stage work because the hero had shouted at them (at the end of Act II): "Till you feed us, right and wrong can wait. . . ." And for the right-wing press Brecht was now stamped with the label "cultural Bolshevist," mainly for his mockery of the Bible and "sacred" institutions, such as family and marriage, and for his blunt exposure of sexual habits and prostitution. His own "Notes to *The Threepenny Opera*," written three years after the Berlin premiere, are, as so often with him, a retrospective attempt to reconcile a previous creation with a theoretical position reached or consolidated afterwards. It is simply not true that "*The Threepenny Opera* is concerned with bourgeois conceptions not only as content, by representing them, but also through the manner in which it does so."[11] Macheath, a kind of Robin Hood and François Villon rolled into one, is motivated and doomed less by notions emanating from the bourgeois class than by Baalian sex appetites and habits stronger than reason or socio-economic factors. His urge to sleep with a woman even at the risk of being caught by the police is comparable to Galy Gay's "arch impulse" to sink his teeth into the enemy's neck. Ironically, it corresponds to some of the most recent theories in zoology and anthropology, which, if sustained by scientific data on a large scale, will strike the death blow to Rousseau's notion regarding the inherently good nature of man—and that means to Marx, as well. Brecht was undoubtedly aware of the doctrinaire shortcomings of his play of 1928, and that is why he tried to provide directions in his notes, which were intended to stress the sociological aspects through the technical devices of his newly formulated epic theater. And that is why he tried to make the subsequent film scenario of *Die Dreigroschenoper* more Marxist and why in the early 1930's he rewrote the story as a novel with Macheath having become a banker.

Many Brecht scholars attribute the writing of the play to the German Handel renaissance in the twenties, which presumably angered the young hater of "culinary" opera. It is true that several of the most obscure of Handel's more than seventy Italian-style operas were revived throughout Germany after 1920, and it is also true that, already in 1728, John Gay had stopped that trend in London and caused Handel to concentrate on oratorios, but to imply that Brecht wanted to do the same thing for our time is to attribute to him a solemn and almost scholarly concern with opera, which was alien to him. It is also unlikely that the success of a London revival of the Gay musical in 1920 should have prompted a German playwright to duplicate that success eight years later. When Brecht's collaborator Elisabeth Hauptmann came upon the English text by chance, she instantly recognized the suitability of the material, and I am satisfied with her answer (when I asked her in 1966): "Don't forget, in those years we often did things because we simply liked to and it was fun doing them." Although it should not be denied that Brecht's theory of the epic theater was partly influenced by a strong dislike of traditional opera, his chief motivation for *Die Dreigroschenoper* was the lewd bawdiness of the old story with its obvious possibilities for contemporary satire. The finished product catered to the flippant and cynical mood of the Weimar Republic in its declining chaotic years. The society presented may be amenable to social change, as is occasionally implied by Brecht; but man, as he sees him, is fundamentally wicked, and Mr. Peachum sums it up in the following irrevocable state-

ment repeated three times: "The world is poor and men are bad /
There is of course no more to add."

VI   Aufstieg und Fall der Stadt Mahagonny
(The Rise and Fall of Mahagonny)

Brecht's collaboration with Weill had already begun before
Die Dreigroschenoper and had resulted in a kind of short ora-
torio based on six Kipling-inspired songs. Known as *Das Kleine
Mahagonny* (The Little Mahagonny), this "song play" was performed at the Baden-Baden Music Festival of 1927. It was probably the sensational success of *Die Dreigroschenoper* that caused
Brecht to expand the earlier work into another full-length assault
upon traditional opera. *Aufstieg und Fall der Stadt Mahagonny*,
however, provoked the loudest scandal in the scandal-rich history of Brecht openings when it was first performed in Leipzig
in 1930. The author attributed its failure to the provincial mentality of bourgeois audiences, which were baffled by seemingly
incoherent stage events and mostly angered by a totally absurdist
closing scene in which the anarchic nature of man is celebrated
by street demonstrators carrying inscriptions such as "For the
natural disorder of things!" and "For the perpetuation of the
Golden Age!" It is true that the more sophisticated Berliners
were less shocked by staged anarchy one year later when real
anarchy had practically become a way of life in the German
capital; but *Aufstieg und Fall der Stadt Mahagonny* never caught
on. Only Weill's music was praised, and Brecht lovers noted that
the libretto contained some of his finest lyrics.

The setting of the work is again a fictitious America. Mrs.
Begbick of *Mann ist Mann* has left her equally fictitious India
and is fleeing from the police with two fellow crooks. They decide to found a new city in which the gold miners will find and
buy their pleasures. Mahagonny, however, does not flourish until
Paul Ackermann from Alaska arrives and teaches them the
secret of success: everything should be permitted. Now they
eat, make love, fight, and drink without reservation. Only one
rule governs: money; and one day Paul is found violating that
rule because he has run out of money. Since nobody, including the
girl he loves, is willing to pay his debts, he is tried and sen-

tenced to death "for lack of money, which is the most hideous crime on this planet." While Mahagonny is burning down in the background, Paul is electrocuted among demonstrating bystanders, who sing after his execution, "We cannot help a dead man. We cannot help ourselves. Nor you. Nor anybody."

Since Brecht's "Notes to *Mahagonny*" (1930) contain his first explicit exposition of the theory of the epic theater and were rewritten from the perspective of Marxist philosophy (which he had not yet fully embraced while writing the opera between 1928 and 1929), many critics include *Aufstieg und Fall der Stadt Mahagonny* among Brecht's communistic works. It is nothing of the kind. It is his most despairing, black, and pessimistic statement about man's unredeemable badness in the form of dramatic satire and using the devices of the Theater of the Absurd. Neither restrictions nor indulgences will benefit humanity, and money does not buy happiness. Jakob, the glutton, eats himself to death; Joe, the boxer, is killed in a fight; and Paul, the only "human" among the disgusting group of pleasure-seekers, is betrayed and executed. Despite Brecht's acquaintance with Marxism since 1926, the opera is, so to speak, the swan song of the metaphysical anarchist before he found the taming discipline of communism for his inner chaos. It seems to me that Brecht goes far beyond symbolizing in his City of Mahagonny the insoluble crisis of capitalism, as some critics have maintained. There is not even a hint of suggestion that humanity could ever change for the better. Bronnen has recently revealed that Brecht first coined the word "Mahagonny" when he observed the brown-shirted Hitler hordes in the Munich of 1923.[12] Now, years later, his broader picture of a nonpolitical utopia was still painted with the same repulsive color of human feces. While, as we will see, the later Brecht was to reach the conclusion that human inequities and economic crises are not as inevitable as storms and earthquakes, but were modifiable, the young dramatist, at the end of his first phase of production, was still pronouncing his nihilism and pessimism through the following unequivocal lines of Mrs. Begbick: "Bad is the hurricane, worse is the typhoon, yet worst is man."

CHAPTER 3

Portrait of the Artist as a Marxist Teacher

BRIGHT, impatient, critical, and indolent students often tend
to become good teachers in later life. Similarly, Wedekind
and Erich Kästner, often labeled immoral for their shock-assaults
upon sacred cows, were, if anything, deeply motivated moralists
who endeavored to teach readers and audiences through the
medium of their art. Brecht was no exception. Not only was
there something of a country schoolmaster about the appearance
of the frugal, short Swabian with the curiously old-fashioned
steel-rimmed glasses, but his intimate friends as well as casual
visitors have often commented on the aura of constant arguing, studying, reading, and learning that surrounded him. As a
theatrical director, the older Brecht increasingly resembled a
professor who conducts seminars in the Socratic method; and his
actors and assistants treated him like a respected teacher. Once
the early chaos of his dramatic apprenticeship "was used up"
(as he had put it in *Im Dickicht der Städte*) and the new platform of a Marxist philosophy had been sufficiently cemented, his
latent schoolmaster inclinations came to the fore, and he used
the theater as an educational forum.

Brecht's so-called *Lehrstücke*, didactic plays which he wrote
between 1928 and 1934, are not basically new. They are merely
modern variations of an old German theatrical form that had
long been forgotten. They go back to the school drama of the
Reformation and of Humanism, which was part of the curricu-
lum in the sixteenth century, since it gave the pupils an opportunity to practice their mastery of Latin—and later of German—
by enhancing memory, elocution, and physical posture. A century later, this type of drama was widely used for the inculcation
of moral, religious (by the Jesuits), and political values. After
the revolution of 1918, the appreciation of art for pedagogical

61

purposes received a new impetus; and painters, poets, and composers concerned themselves with the functional aspects of their crafts as the aims of the Bauhaus Movement and the terms *Gebrauchslyrik* (Kästner) and *Gebrauchsmusik* (Hindemith) clearly demonstrate. It is likely that Brecht's association with composers such as Hindemith, Weill, and Eisler, which had originated in a joint rejection of traditional opera, made him interested in a new simplistic, austere type of drama that did not require a costly apparatus and could be staged by lay actors and directors. Other sources were the new medium of the radio, which offered a challenge to young playwrights, and the Oriental theater, especially the Japanese No-plays in the English translation by Arthur Waley which Brecht got to know through his collaborator Elisabeth Hauptmann. Last but not least, the secret schoolmaster felt the urge to expound his new Marxism in a manner that would not only satisfy his own skeptical mind but teach others as well.

The first of the didactic plays, *Der Flug der Lindberghs* (The Flight of the Lindberghs), with music by Hindemith and Weill, is, essentially, a glorification of scientific progress and an affirmation of atheism: disorder is attributed to ignorance, and God becomes the source of all evil. To avoid the charge of hero-worship and to emphasize his new anti-individualism, Brecht presented the famous flyer as a chorus: a collective image of the new man who braves fog and snowstorms and who overcomes weariness and sleep. Despite a short reference to "dialectic economics which will change the world fundamentally," the transformation of society is not yet the concern of this short play, which rather concerns the conquest of nature.[1] Although specifically intended as an educational exercise for boys and girls, *Der Flug der Lindberghs* received only one radio production and a few concert performances, including one by the Philadelphia Orchestra under Leopold Stokowski in 1931. In *Das Badener Lehrstück vom Einverständnis* (The Didactic Play of Baden-Baden on Consent), Brecht went one step beyond his previous pseudo-materialism and wrote a kind of sequel to the challenge of nature by shifting the issue to man's social relations. Four airmen have crashed and are close to death. Two choirs representing mankind debate whether or not the men deserve help. Their deliberations are aided by photos showing men killed by men in our time and an absurd scene during which two clowns "cure" a third one of his pains by sawing off his limbs and, finally, even his head. Thus, the conclusion is: man does not help man; power, not help, is what matters until our world is changed. Violence must be combated with violence. Man's function is to be useful to others, and the flyers are no longer useful. Three of the men accept the verdict with humility and consent to their death; they are redeemed by the tribunal, whereas the pilot Charles Nungesser, who did not fly for anyone but only for the sake of flying and for glory (Charles Lindbergh), is condemned with the words: "Die then, you-who-are-no-longer-a-man!" Produced at the Baden-Baden Music Festival of 1929, the play—or, as it is often called, the cantata—was performed in several cities and on Brussels radio in 1934. Spectators fainted during the grotesque and absurd scene in which a man's limbs are sawed off by three clowns in order to demonstrate that man does not help man. This scene also resulted in quarrels with Hindemith, who had composed the music, and it impaired Brecht's collaboration with him.

Given Brecht's personality, with its anarchic tendencies, it is clear that the problem of submission fascinated and plagued him more than any other, once he believed he had found in Marxism a new sustaining philosophy of life. Therefore, he pursued the problem of consent (or acquiescence) still more sharply in his next "school opera." *Der Jasager* (He Who Says Yes) (music by Weill), based on a short fifteenth-century No-play, *Tamiko*, tells us of a boy who joins an expedition through the mountains which his teacher undertakes in order to procure medicine against an epidemic. When the boy gets sick, his companions must either abandon him or turn back. According to "an old custom," the boy consents to be left behind for the sake of the community but asks to be killed rather than face a slow death. The companions comply, "deploring the sad turn of events, no one more guilty than his neighbor." The play was widely performed in schools and hailed by bourgeois and Catholic critics for its unequivocal espousal of the Christian (or Prussian) ethics of sacrifice. Only the pupils of a Marxist school in Berlin objected to the solution, and Brecht responded by rewriting the end and calling the little opera *Der Neinsager* (He Who Says No). Now the members of the expedition turn back and bring the child to safety:

> side by side, they walked close together
> to face the blame
> to face the laughter, their eyes tightly shut,
> no one more cowardly than his neighbor.

There is no question in my mind that Brecht did not agree with the harsh solution of the first version (which would well have served the ethics of Nazi elite schools and Kamikaze flyers a decade later), but wanted to elicit critical responses, and that he stated his own newly gained position in the second version: "Rather what I need is a new custom which we are going to institute without delay: the custom of freshly thinking through each new situation." It must, however, be conceded that Brecht cheated somewhat by doing away with the unequivocal character of the conflict. There is no epidemic in the second version; the expedition is simply a scientific one, and there is no earthly reason why the boy ought to be abandoned. It seems that Brecht was not yet ready to face the grim question of whether the end justifies the means. This he did in his next play.

I   Die Massnahme
(The Measures Taken)

Four political agitators have returned from an illegal mission to China and report the liquidation of a young communist who had endangered their assignment. The "control chorus" (symbolizing the conscience and judgment of the Party) agrees to render its verdict for the measures they have taken, whereupon the four agents (three men and one woman) enact the mistakes of the young comrade, each, in turn, playing his part. It appears that he violated specific orders on four successive occasions, and thus brought the mission to the brink of failure. Out of compassion and emotional sympathy, the young communist delayed the revolt of exploited coolies by trying to alleviate their plight; he frustrated the Party's propaganda work by attacking a policeman during a strike; he broke off negotiations with a greedy capitalist, deemed useful for tactical reasons, because he was revolted by the man; and, finally, he led a premature uprising which, in turn, disclosed his identity as a foreign agent. Since the continuation of the mission depended on remaining unrecognized and no possibility existed to smuggle him out of the country, the four emissaries decided to kill him. He himself confessed his errors and consented to their decision. They shot him and threw his body into a lime pit, so that no trace of it would remain. The control chorus absolves the four agitators and agrees with the measures taken.

The uncompromising harshness of Brecht's treatment has bestowed a great deal of notoriety on this play, which is usually considered the most obvious proof of his association with communism. It also ended the playwright's collaboration with Hindemith and Weill, caused his break with the "new music," since a requested production at the Baden-Baden Festival was rejected, and started his working relationship with the communist Hanns Eisler, who composed the austere score. The only German performances of the work took place in Berlin with the participation of workers' choirs in 1930 and 1931. The fact that the older Brecht, after his return to East Berlin, did not authorize any new productions, has also led to speculations and unflattering comments. By that time, the Stalinistic purge trials of the thirties had provided ample illustrations to all kinds of "measures taken," and it seemed quite evident that a play that had already caused considerable embarrassment to the Party in 1930 would not be exonerated in Ulbricht's Germany. It seems to me, however, that neither the evasive argumentation of communist critics nor the malevolent smugness of most Western scholars has been responsive to the true significance of *Die Massnahme,* which may be one of the genuine tragedies of our time.

That the Party was not exactly thrilled by a theatrical exhibition of murder sanctioned for political reasons should not be surprising. It was all the more painful, since Brecht was a famous fellow traveler who supported its cause at a time when other bourgeois writers either abstained from politics or even succumbed to the growing danger of German fascism. His embarrassing play was still more aggravating because the killed comrade was a compassionate idealist on whom the sympathies of audiences and readers were focused. Communist reviewers generally solved the dilemma by respectfully blaming the playwright's lack of practice of, and participation in, communism, which had resulted in a mechanical or "vulgar" Marxism not yet dialectic. They tried to show that, even in Lenin's terms, the young comrade was more often right than wrong, and, furthermore, that the Party's severest punishment was expulsion rather than death. Contemporary Marxist critics and scholars still take essentially the same position and reject the abstractness of the situations which, they claim, deprived Brecht's play of "the lively complexity of reality." Western critics, on the other hand, either gleefully see in *Die Massnahme* an anticipation of the confession trials of the Stalinist era or an attempt by a cruel author to teach audiences the need for inhumanity by hook or by crook.

It is, of course, true that the young Brecht of 1930 lacked both a profound grasp of communist theory and tactics and an intimate contact with the proletariat. He was, and remained, an intellectual fellow traveler. Although he had been reading some of Marx's writings since 1926 and for a while had even attended courses in an adult school for workers, he did not pursue his studies in the systematic fashion of a student of political science. From the Marxist sociologist Fritz Sternberg, a critic of the German Communist Party to whom Brecht gave a copy of *Mann ist Mann* with the inscription "To my first real teacher," we know that Brecht was essentially motivated by compassion and that his theoretical studies remained sporadic and superficial.[2] If he took from Marx and Lenin (and later from Mao) some basic ideas that seemed to confirm, and correspond to, notions and experiences of his own, he only did what creative artists usually do. Are Western critics unduly bothered by Goethe's ambiguous Christianity? Are Schiller and Kleist inferior poets because they tried to adapt Kant to their aesthetic needs rather than follow him to the letter? To judge a dramatist and poet by the degree of literal adherence to the thinkers who informed him is no more sensible and justified than to evaluate a scientist on the basis of his religious beliefs or sexual practices. Moreover, such a fundamental misunderstanding of the nature of literature usually leads to moral judgments entirely dependent on the platform of the viewer. Communist critics may correctly argue that the measures taken by Brecht's agitators were in violation of Party tactics even according to Lenin—but they miss the boat, so to speak, since the playwright's concern was not political but moral or even metaphysical. On the other hand, Western scholars, even today, refuse to concede the existence of measures equally "inhuman," and often more terrible than those described in Brecht's play, outside of the discipline of the Party. It seems to me that the conflict in *Die Massnahme* has actually gained in disturbing relevance since 1930, a fact, incidentally, which may very well be the real reason why the aging dramatist refused to authorize further performances after the war. A thoroughly convinced Marxist, one who had by then come to deny the possibility of modern tragedy in the age of progressive science, he mut have been deeply disturbed that he had written one against his intentions.

When Mr. Peachum sang in *Die Dreigroschenoper,* "We would be good, instead of base, / But this old world is not that kind of place," he at least implied that, one day, the world might become that kind of place. Again and again, Brecht occupied himself with the inherent question of whether or not goodness is possible, or, differently stated, whether or not man can be good and live at all. The more he studied Marx, the more he came to realize that individual morality might have to be changed or at least temporarily suspended while mankind effects the transition to a better world. The last lines of Brecht's most moving poem ("An die Nachgeborenen" [To Posterity]) eloquently state what he considered to be the cruel dilemma of our time:

> Alas, we
> Who wished to lay the foundations of kindness
> Could not ourselves be kind.
>
> But you, when at last it comes to pass
> That man can help his fellow man,
> Do not judge us
> Too harshly.[3]

By 1930, the despair and cynicism of *Die Dreigroschenoper* and *Mahagonny* had been replaced by Brecht's hope that the discipline of a Marx-oriented collective would eventually do for human society what the discipline of science had accomplished in the conquest of nature by "making the world almost inhabitable." The first prerequisite in this endeavor would be the shedding of excessive individualistic fat, as it were. If, as every obese person knows, it is difficult to lose weight, why should we assume that the process of spiritual and moral reducing would be less painful? The didactic plays of Brecht are, therefore, exercises in the adjustment of the so-called personality of our time, shaped by idealistic and bourgeois concepts, to the less individualistic man of the future, guided by the needs of the collective. To the moralist Brecht, the most crucial and difficult part of the job at hand presented itself in the problem of submission to discipline.

Die Massnahme provokes reactions of extreme discomfort and moral indignation precisely because it reveals the problematic character of individual goodness. The real tragic heroes are the agitators who are compelled to act against their individual feeling and code of ethics. Those critics who condemn the acquittal by the control chorus must also reject all acquiescence in similar barbarism elsewhere; they should not only point at the Soviet purge trials Brecht presumably anticipated but must equally abhor the intelligence and spy activities of organizations such as the CIA, and they cannot possibly condone the dropping of the atom bomb or wars such as the ones in Southeast Asia. As a matter of fact, the last two examples reveal an even greater degree of inhumanity because they lack the consent of the participants, in contrast to Brecht's communists, who knowingly accept their mission with all moral risks involved. In a ritual called by the playwright "The Blotting Out," they symbolically extinguish their individual personalities before entering Manchuria, and the leader asks: "Then you are ready to die and to hide the dead ones?" Whereupon the men answer: "Yes." And he tells them: "Then you are yourselves no longer." The control chorus absolves the agents from the tenets of traditional ethics: "Who fights for communism must be able to fight and not to fight; to speak the truth and not to speak the truth; to perform services and not to perform services; to keep promises and not to keep promises; to go into danger and to keep out of danger;

to be recognizable and not to be recognizable. Who fights for communism possesses only one of the virtues: that he fights for communism."

In 1930 it was possible to see in those lines the cruel and perhaps even cynical justification for fanatic conspirators, and some critics were quick to point out that the above description would also fit the hideous murders by right-wing semisecret organizations in the Germany of the twenties. In the meantime, the world has witnessed mass genocide in the name of racial purification, slave labor and concentration camps for either world domination or enforced industrialization, and wars inflicted on unwilling natives, so that "they may decide their own destiny." Today the words of the control chorus not only characterize illegal conspirators but could easily serve as a loyalty oath for "legitimate" agencies of almost any country. The erosion of public morality has only brought into sharper focus what is perhaps the dominant problem of human ethics in modern times. For Brecht it was a central conflict to which he returned again and again, though never in the uncompromising constellation of the men in *Die Massnahme*. That spontaneous compassion, sympathy, and goodness may conflict with overriding principles (or long-range goals) is by no means only a problem of political tactics but a genuine manifestation of the human condition. In broad philosophical terms, the young comrade does not act differently from Heinrich von Kleist's Prince of Homburg, who defies specific orders that he, as an officer, was sworn to obey. German professors who rave about the "humanity" of his commanding officer, the Prussian Elector, because he lifts the death sentence when the Prince finally realizes the severity of his offense, should rather ponder the question of whether or not the Elector would also have pardoned an officer whose disobedience had lost him the battle. Even a universally revered figure such as Churchill can be seen in the same predicament, as Rolf Hochhuth has attempted to show in his controversial play *The Soldiers* (1967).[4] In short, the four agitators and the comrade find themselves in the same position as any tragic hero who is torn between a code of ethics and his personal passions and inclinations, or, differently expressed, between individual and collective morality. It is likely that the Brecht of the early 1930's believed with Marx that the conflict would disappear with the passage of time, i.e., with the victory of a transformed society, and that is why he condemned in the young comrade his own individual compassion, so to speak. He did not intend to write a tragedy because the progress of mankind, implied by Marxian dialectics, is essentially optimistic and rules out the possibility of tragedy, which is reduced to a mistake that could have been avoided. It seems to me that Brecht became doubtful in his later years as to whether or not the ethical conflict of *Die Massnahme* could ever be eliminated by the dialectic of human history. If it was, in fact, unsolvable, he must have come to the painful conclusion that he had written a tragedy against his will.

II   Die heilige Johanna der Schlachthöfe
(Saint Joan of the Stockyards)

It is understandable that a bursting dramatic talent as explorative and protean as Brecht's would not forever remain chained to the restrictive fetters of his didactic plays, which are more like the études of a composer occasionally found among his major sonatas and symphonies. As long as Brecht was grappling with a new philosophy (Marxism) and a new form (the epic theater), he apparently felt the need for self-clarification through exercises, while the teacher in him simultaneously wished to demonstrate the impact of his newly gained position as concisely and simply as possible for the benefit of others. Once Brecht was secure in his Marxist humanism, his austere didacticism mellowed with the normal process of artistic maturing. Moreover, for a while the new foe, Hitlerism, consumed most of his polemic energies, and the circumstances of his exile took away any chance for lay productions by German pupils or workers, thus rendering the primary function of the *Lehrstücke* obsolete.

While the last of Brecht's didactic plays *Die Horatier und die Kuriatier* (The Horatians and the Curiatians [1934]), turned out to be an uncommonly arid exercise in dialectic strategy and tactics motivated by antifascism, he still followed the ethical conflict of *Die Massnahme* with another demonstration of the precariousness of human kindness. *Die Ausnahme und die Regel* (The Exception and the Rule [1930]), effectively shows that our world, i.e., capitalism according to Marx, has perverted moral values. A merchant in the desert, trying to beat his competitor, shoots an overworked and abused coolie who is trying to offer him a drink of water. The merchant has mistaken the bottle for a weapon. At a subsequent trial, he is acquitted because he acted in self-defense. He had every reason to assume that, given the circumstances, the coolie would harm him (the rule) and not help him (the exception). Esslin calls this parable on class justice "that most bitter of all of Brecht's plays," but I disagree. The merchant did not *have* to kill the coolie, and the whole tone of the play suggests the transitory character of society in which what is now the rule may one day become the exception provided we, the spectators, will learn from the demonstration. The closing lines make this very clear:

> What here's the rule, recognize as an abuse
> And where you have recognized an abuse
> Provide a remedy!

Anger at a world that condones the evil actions of an evil man may be a strong emotion and even release an equally strong will toward change (undoubtedly the playwright's intention), but to Brecht "the most bitter" of all possible conflicts presented itself in the opposite constellation: the good man torn between his natural inclination toward kindness or his individual moral code and the demands of overriding principles or collective needs. In *Die Massnahme*, he had explored the plight of committed man (even at the risk of writing a modern classical tragedy); but of greater relevance to him always was and remained the problem of the less committed person, as doubting and skeptical as he found himself; and he tackled that problem in *Die heilige Johanna der Schlachthöfe* (Saint Joan of the Stockyards [1928–29]), his first full-length Marxist play.

The new drama—the longest Brecht ever wrote—is, to a certain degree, the autobiographical story of the bourgeois author's involvement with the proletariat and his gradual acceptance of violence. Joan Dark, an evangelist for "the Black Straw Hats," tries to alleviate the misery of the workers in the stockyards of Chicago. Her chief antagonist is Pierpont Mauler, king of the

meat-packers, whose market manipulations cause economic crises and mass unemployment. Joan pleads with him to reopen
the factories, and he is touched by her innocence without,
however, really helping her. Thrown out by the Black Straw
Hats, who depend on the support of the meat-packers, who, in
turn, need them to divert the poor from their plight, Joan joins
the unemployed. She helps to organize a general strike, but
fails to deliver a crucial letter to the other workers of the city
when she realizes that violence must be used. The strike fails.
Joan, sick from cold and starvation, collapses and is dying.
With her last strength, she proclaims a new belief in the necessity of violence. The meat-packers and the Straw Hats, however, are drowning out her words because they realize that the
girl would make a useful martyr. While Joan vainly denounces
both the economic system and religion which prevent man from
helping himself, she is canonized as Saint Joan of the Stockyards.

Some scholars attribute Brecht's motivation for writing this
play to the five hundredth anniversary of Jeanne d'Arc's death
in 1931, which was bound to irritate him. It seems unlikely to
me that such an event should have prompted the author to start
on a project two years before it was due. If we must seek a
specific historical occasion, the centennial of William Booth in
1929 would suggest a more meaningful anniversary, especially
since we know that Brecht and his friends roamed the soup
kitchens of the Salvation Army during the depression in Berlin.
Moreover, his documented admiration for George Bernard Shaw
seems to indicate that he got some of his motives from both
Major Barbara and *Saint Joan,* the latter play having had a
spectacular production under Max Reinhardt in 1924, the rehearsals for which Brecht attended. As to the girl from Lorraine,
she apparently held a special, lifelong fascination for Brecht:
during the war she reappeared in *Die Gesichte der Simone
Machard* (The Visions of Simone Machard), written with Feuchtwanger's collaboration, and in East Berlin he later adapted and
staged a version of the Rouen Trial, written by Anna Seghers.
In addition, there was Schiller's bombastic classic, *The Maid
of Orleans,* which Brecht detested and which offered itself as a
fitting object for his love of parody. Whatever the exact reasons
for attempting the first major drama in his new "classical" style,

Brecht seems to have considered the material ideally suited for an infusion with the spirit of Marxism and for adapting it to the form of his new epic theater.

In a way, *Die heilige Johanna der Schlachthöfe* concludes Brecht's education in Marxism, which had commenced in 1926 while he was working on a play, *Joe Fleischhacker*, set in Chicago, inspired by Upton Sinclair, and dealing with "the incomprehensible fluctuations" of the wheat market. Another unfinished play, *Der Brotladen* (The Bread Shop), dealt with the same topic. The Salvation Army motive was added by Brecht's collaborator Elisabeth Hauptmann, who wrote (jointly with him) a musical, *Happy End*, with music by Kurt Weill, which flopped miserably in 1929. In the meantime, the workings of the stock market had indeed become comprehensible to the student of Marx, and in *Die heilige Johanna der Schlachthöfe* they even provide the structure of the play. As some critics have shown, the thirteen scenes (eleven in Bentley's translation) follow the cycle of a capitalistic crisis as Marx has described it in the twenty-third chapter of the first book of his *Kapital*.[5] Joan, driven by compassion and the desire to help the poor, fails because she does not understand the economic system under which she lives. Mauler, her opponent, is also caught in the system because he realizes that, were he to change, he would only be replaced by somebody else; and so he is forced to go on with a life that is distasteful to him but that will make him richer and more powerful. Brecht's greatness lies in his ability to make the basic conflict human and universally appealing, irrespective of any ideological platform. Just as we do not have to share Shakespeare's concept of Elizabethan feudalism in order to be moved by his tragedies, one can appreciate *Die heilige Johanna der Schlachthöfe* without underwriting Brecht's Marxist description of capitalist society. The fact that, in many significant details, modern capitalism has not developed according to the expectations of Marx does not invalidate Joan's conflict between individual goodness and its temporary suspension for the sake of a higher goal.

Both communist and Western scholars criticize Brecht's seeming shift in this play from socioeconomic factors to religion. The Marxist critic Ernst Schumacher deplores the author's

unfamiliarity with the practices of the proletariat that has
presumably caused the playwright to mount an attack against
religion rather than the bloodless "reformism" of ineffective
groups such as the German socialists, for instance. The British
scholar Ronald Gray sees Joan as an "emotional socialist" and
condemns her for hysterical intolerance (and her creator for
"gratuitous sadism") because her last words are not directed
against the evils of capitalism but against a belief in God.[6] The
answer is, of course, that Brecht did not deny the possibility of
God's existence but rather attacked the manipulation of organized religion for purposes of preserving social injustice. He
took Marx's dictum of "opium for the people" literally: a narcotic
will soothe pain for a while but will transform the user into an
addict whose mental and physical powers may deteriorate to the
point of dependence upon the drug; the result will be total
inaction. Joan condemns herself at the end for having helped
the cause of the meat-packers because she cultivated a

> goodness without consequences! Intentions in the dark!
> I have changed nothing.
> Vanishing fruitless from this world
> I say to you:
> Take care that when you leave the world
> You were not only good but are leaving
> A good world!

It is, however, significant that even while she curses those who
proclaim "a God who can be invisible and yet help them," she
explicitly holds man responsible for bringing his house into
disorder:

> And the lowness of those above is measureless
> And even if they improve that would be
> No help, because the system they have made
> is unique: exploitation
> And disorder, bestial and therefore
> Incomprehensible.

In short, Brecht's thesis is that the "incomprehensibility" of
the world is prolonged by the use—or misuse—of religion; and

while an ignorant girl like Joan cannot possibly grasp the economic intricacies of the capitalist system, she—and that means everybody—can be brought to the realization that such ignorance is self-imposed and untenable. If Joan had simply proclaimed that "God helps only those who help themselves," the substance of Brecht's play would be unchanged.

Joan's long and painful road toward the acceptance of force illustrates her creator's equally painful effort to overcome his own inherited bourgeois scruples and softness. As late as the ninth scene, and in the midst of machine-gun fire, she says:

I'm leaving. What's done by force cannot be good. I don't belong with them. If hunger and the tread of misery had taught me violence as a child, I would belong to them and ask no questions. But as it is, I must leave.

But she is as little able to leave as Brecht was able to deny the necessity of Marxist class struggle, despite his mental reservations and despite the fact that he did not "belong to them." On May 1, 1929, when German communists demonstrated in Berlin, Brecht observed from a window of Fritz Sternberg's apartment how the police fired into the unarmed crowd and killed several persons. Sternberg reports that he had never seen Brecht's face as white before, and that this experience, more than any other, had probably driven the playwright into the arms of the communists.[7] There is no question in my mind that the event found its literary counterpart in *Die heilige Johanna der Schlachthöfe*, which, to a certain extent, may therefore be called an autobiographical play. Pierpont Mauler, Joan's antagonist, on the other hand, is a composite of personality traits the young author imagined a great capitalistic tycoon would possess. He is shrewd, ruthless, cynical, deceitful, and sentimental at the same time. He is not a monster, but the most human of meatpackers, which speaks for Brecht's sense of artistic balance. If, nevertheless, the work suffers from a certain abstractness which seems to have adversely affected a fuller characterization of all minor figures, and even of Joan herself, this is due to the playwright's groping for a new style, the full mastery of which he was only gradually to attain.

Die heilige Johanna der Schlachthöfe is Brecht's first verse drama in a grand manner, as it were. There had been songs and occasional lyrics before, and he had tried out a new technique of unrhymed verse in his didactic plays, but he had never attempted a poetic full-length drama. Brecht's "grand manner" is an unrhymed verse with irregular rhythms, which he defined more precisely in an essay ten years later[8] and about which we will have to say more in Chapter 7. Prose dialogue still remains, but is now mainly reserved for the handling of minor plot incidents or for contrast between rhythmical passages, while Schiller's blank verse and Goethe's shorter rhymed verse from *Faust* deliberately parody German idealism. The ironic effect is enhanced by Brecht's employment of classical meter in a satirical sense precisely at those spots where German tradition demands noble sentiments and spiritual enhancement. Thus, the slaughter of an ox and the manufacture of canned pork are described in pure blank verse, and Joan's canonization takes place in a setting paralleling Schiller's *Maid of Orleans* while choruses chant verses closely structured after the closing lines of the redemption scene in Goethe's *Faust II*. Brecht's hatred of a shallow bourgeois pseudo-idealism had led him to a simplistic equation of German classicism with feudalism, which, although unjustified in general, may readily be noted in Schiller's heroine. That a playwright as famous as Brecht was by 1931 could not find a theater for his drama two years before Hitler's rise to power might have been due not only to the growing right-wing political climate in Germany but also to the indirect assault upon the two most revered names in German literature, a sacrilege making Brecht eligible for the epithet "cultural Bolshevist." The play remained unperformed until 1959; only a few scenes were broadcast by the Berlin Radio in 1932.

III Die Mutter
(The Mother)

There is general agreement that Brecht came closest to being a communist writer with the dramatization of Maxim Gorky's famous novel *The Mother*. The book by the Russian author, written between 1905 and 1907, had long become an international classic of proletarian literature, and in 1927 a Soviet film based on it had focused new attention on the celebrated work. Here was a novel by one of the few truly great practitioners of "socialist realism," who had told the story of a simple revolutionary woman and who had himself returned to Russia after many years of residence abroad; the material was ideal for a communist playwright. The result was a work which, although approved by the Party more than other Brechtian efforts, never attained unqualified praise or popularity in the East and is usually slighted as a piece of propaganda by Western critics. It has, however, much to recommend it to the unbiased lover of literature, and must be considered one of Brecht's major plays. The central character, Pelagea Vlassova, is a kind of precursor of the richly executed and complex stage figures of Brecht's late period, such as Mother Courage and Galileo. She is sly, shrewd, stubborn, dignified, humorous, heroic, and, most of all, brimming over with vitality. Hostile to the revolutionary movement at first, Pelagea is gradually drawn into it to protect her son Pavel. She distributes leaflets, takes part in a demonstration during which he is arrested, learns to read, helps striking peasants, converts neighbors, operates a printing press; and after Pavel has been shot while escaping from Siberia, she becomes even more determined and continues the fight for the revolution.

It is clear that Brecht did not aim at transferring Gorky, who had the plot of his novel end in 1905, faithfully to the stage. He used an already existing dramatization by two German fellow writers, but rewrote it entirely. Only seven of his fourteen scenes correspond more or less to the Russian model, and the events are carried to the eve of the October Revolution of 1917. There is as much—or as little—historical Russia in the play as there is Germany, and the "Report on May first, 1905" (fifth scene) corresponds more to the demonstration of May 1, 1929, which Brecht watched in Berlin and which had already left its literary trace in *Die heilige Johanna der Schlachthöfe*.[9] Brecht adapted the material to his needs. He had come as close to the proletariat in the Berlin of 1930 as he was ever to come, and he wanted to entertain simple people with the story of an exemplary simple person everybody could identify with. He wanted to teach revolutionary behavior, its beginnings and development, by way of a story that would also appeal to bourgeois audiences; and he wanted to apply the concepts of his newly formulated epic theater. While Gorky's Pelagea retains a typically Russian religiosity, Brecht's Mother has learned from Joan Dark's mistake, so to speak, and her atheism (not militant but rather ironical) has become a prerequisite for transformation to an active revolutionary. At a time when right-wing militarism and secret rearmament were no longer threats but living realities in the Weimar Republic, the German playwright needed a heroine who would also be a pacifist; this is the reason why Brecht's Pelagea carries her fight into the First World War. As a matter of fact, the most effective (and amusing) scene shows her confusing a number of middle-class women who line up to make contributions of scrap metal to the Russian war effort. Brecht must have remembered many similar scenes from Augsburg when he was a boy.

It may be asked what makes *Die Mutter* different from Brecht's didactic plays, especially since some scholars have called it a *Lehrstück*. Brecht himself referred to it as "written in the style of the didactic plays, but requiring professional actors." It will be recalled that all of his didactic plays were short, usually demonstrations of decisions the protagonists had taken under clearly defined circumstances. They were intended for lay actors and did not require acting skills, since no character development over an extended period of time was involved. *Die Mutter* differs in this respect because its central theme is Pelagea's gradual transformation from a middle-aged illiterate woman driven by maternal instinct to a self-taught old revolutionary motivated by reason. Moreover, the fourteen scenes of the play (fifteen in the American edition) cover a period of twelve years and follow a narrative pattern, i.e., they are chronological rather than dramatic in the traditional sense. Each scene is presented for its inherent unique or historical value and not as a necessary ingredient to produce a preconceived result or "solution." *Die Mutter* is Brecht's first chronicle play in the new epic form, which he brought to greater perfection with *Galilei* and *Mutter Courage* a decade later. Written in stylized prose with lyrical choral interludes, the drama, despite the wonderfully warm, appealing, and touching protagonist, still suffers from didactic rigidity, because in those years its creator was too preoccupied with his role as a Marxist teacher. *Die Mutter* was the last Brecht play to be performed in Germany (1932) before his exile. The police soon interfered and only allowed platform readings without scenery, costumes, and acting. An American production (undertaken in 1935 by the Civic Repertory Theater of New York), which Brecht attended, provoked his objections to both the translation and the traditionally realistic style of staging. The rehearsals turned into a traumatic experience for everybody involved, and the playwright, screaming invectives in broken English at the bewildered cast, was finally barred from the theater altogether.[10] Although *Die Mutter* lasted for thirty-six performances, critical reaction was mostly negative and, at best, lukewarm. It is interesting to note that the older Brecht, when he produced the play in his own theater in 1951 (with his wife, Helene Weigel, in the title role), felt the need to add a new character: a mature revolutionary, as shrewd and wise as Pelagea. Brecht thus made the play at once more dramatic and less subject to the charge of hero-worship, since the Mother now was no longer surrounded only by young and less effective revolutionaries. Brecht apparently took to heart earlier Party criticism that, by and large, his workers in the play were the least interesting characters. He refused, however, to call the enemies of the proletariat wicked capitalists or to tag them with the customary labels of realistic propaganda. When the audience applauded lines such as "When the rulers have spoken / The ruled will speak," the Ulbricht regime could by no means be sure for whom the applause was intended. Brecht's "formalism" was tolerated only because he was world-famous by then.

IV   Die Tage der Commune
(The Days of the Commune)

Western critics who see in Brecht a great dramatist despite the unfortunate involvement with Marxism which he presumably outgrew in the late 1930's, have little or nothing to say about *Die Tage der Commune* (The Days of the Commune). Unknown to the Anglo-Saxon world,[11] this play refutes the wishful theory about a young anarchic existentialist who moved on to a relatively short middle period of Marxism in order to reach finally a higher plateau of "universal" appeal in his third phase. The facts are that Brecht, having left the United States, and while arranging for his permanent return to Germany, spent his Zurich waiting period (1948–49) writing a historical drama about the only recorded case of a dictatorship of the proletriat before 1918. It turned out to be the last original Brechtian play, his subsequent efforts being adaptations of the works of others or revisions of his own older dramas for production in East Berlin. In other words, the artist remained a Marxist teacher to the very end and that is why we must consider the play in this chapter.

In his book *The Civil War in France*, Marx had elevated those few months of 1871 during which Paris was defended against the Germans by representatives of the lower classes to the status of a classless communist society which, however briefly, came into being at one time and could, therefore, serve as a classic case for the study of political power. He deliberately created a "Commune-Myth" which was intended to serve as a model for his political theory. His friend Engels later conceded that Marx had presented more or less subconscious tendencies of the Commune as conscious plans. In point of historical fact, the rise of the common people in besieged Paris was due to extraordinary circumstances and the majority of the Commune was not motivated by socialist doctrine. What was seen by Marx as the emergence of a classless society within a provisional state that would gradually disappear later served Lenin and Stalin as a historical example for claiming increased powers for the state. Thus, the rise of the Commune has become the classic case for studying the mechanics of revolution with particular emphasis on the problem of force. It was almost inevitable that a playwright who thought of himself as a faithful Marxist, and who had been deeply plagued by the dilemma of sanctioned violence, would sooner or later get around to dramatizing the fateful events in the Paris of 1871.

During his Danish exile, Brecht became acquainted with *The Defeat*, a play about the Commune by the Norwegian writer Nordahl Grieg, which must have impressed him because he published the German translation (by his collaborator Margarete Steffin) in the Moscow-based magazine *Das Wort*. What caused Brecht, more than ten years later, to attempt (or finish?) a "counterplay" is not known yet, but in the preface to *Die Tage der Commune* he freely admitted that some features and characters were adapted from Grieg's play. Could it be that the lifelong schoolmaster who had seen the failure of the 1918 German revolution through weakness and had observed the perversion through force of the Russian revolution in which his Pelagea Vlassowa had once believed wished to give to his compatriots a truly objective play that would teach them the wisdom of Marx as he saw it? I believe that something like this must have prompted the Brecht of 1948 when it became obvious that again no revolution had taken place or was to take place in Germany. Subsequently, in neither of the two emerging German states was there any love for Brecht's play: no performance took place in West Germany, and it was not until the time of his death in 1956 that a few East German productions were authorized.

Die Tage der Commune is as little a revolutionary play as is Gerhart Hauptmann's *The Weavers,* which is still recognized as one of the great social dramas in world literature, although the German Social Democrats of 1892 were disappointed by its gloomy outcome. Just as the uprising of the Silesian weavers had failed, so did the Commune, and it is not surprising that the Ulbricht regime regarded the tendency of the play as "defeatist." Like Hauptmann, who presented an accurate account based on painstaking historical research, Brecht followed the recorded events, and the Marxist scholar Hans Kaufmann claims to have traced more than fifty direct quotations from the text to primary and secondary sources alone.[12] It is apparent that Brecht wished to correct Grieg's slightly romanticized picture of the Commune, and we are reminded that most of his "counterplays" had been provoked by a similar desire, as early as in *Baal* and as recently as in *Heilige Johanna.* He invented a few characters of his own, to be sure, and did not aim at photographic veracity; but he more or less presented the Commune through the same group of Parisians as Grieg had. By alternating between a few street corners in Montmartre and the Paris City Council, his carefully chosen characters portray the formation, the hopes, and the final collapse of the Commune brought about by Thiers and Bismarck. Brecht's play also follows Hauptmann's *Weavers* in the often noted aesthetic device of foregoing an individual hero. There are no main protagonists or leading characters, but a composite of the people emerges as a kind of collective hero. It must, however, be stated that Brecht achieved neither the three-dimensional depth of characterization nor the atmospheric density of the older German dramatist. Some of the little people of the Commune are sentimentalized, while the villains Thiers and Bismarck remain flat caricatures. It is possible, of course, that Brecht would have improved the play had he lived to see the production through and could have profited from rehearsals as was his custom.

In the absence of authentic information concerning the writing of *Die Tage der Commune*, we may assume that Brecht's aim was—still or again—didactic. By putting on the stage the objectively presented story of the only dictatorship of the proletariat in history, he could teach audiences to learn from the dramatic demonstration. Although the Paris Commune of 1871 and the German revolution of 1918 had failed, the people might finally come to master the problem of force and discipline. That the play will aid them in this task seems, however, doubtful. The man who thought of himself as a student and teacher of Marxism never unequivocally resolved the conflict between goodness and violence to his own satisfaction.

CHAPTER 4

Terror and Misery of the Third Reich

IN his testimony before the House Committee on Un-American Activities on October 30, 1947, Brecht replied to a question about the revolutionary character of his writing with the following words: "I have written a number of poems and songs and plays in the fight against Hitler and, of course they can therefore be considered revolutionary because I, of course, was for the overthrow of that government."[1] Although he was obviously trying to minimize his communist identification, the statement nevertheless accurately assesses the motivations for a great many of his creative efforts between 1931 and 1944. Especially in the years immediately following his flight from Germany, Brecht mercilessly fought fascism with his pen. He untiringly contributed to refugee periodicals in Amsterdam, Prague, Paris, and Moscow, as well as to German shortwave broadcasts from Switzerland, London, and the USSR. Appropriate recognition followed in due time: already in 1935 he was officially deprived of his German citizenship by the Nazi government. With Thomas and Heinrich Mann, Bertolt Brecht shared the honor of being the most militant and effective literary spokesman of the "other" Germany. Like Thomas Mann, who could rarely bring himself to refer to Hitler by name but just called him "Der Mensch," Brecht, scornfully mocking the German dictator's known "artistic" inclinations, always called him the house-painter or paperhanger. Although the literary value of Brecht's anti-Nazi output is probably not as high as that of some of his other work, critics tend to downgrade or neglect it unduly. It is also often impossible to distinguish between procommunist and antifascist motivations in the case of an author who freely admitted to both tendencies. It may be said that, by and large, the more urgent task of fighting Hitler and his mad regime consumed most of

Brecht's creative energies in the earlier years of his exile and—
to a lesser degree—continued to occupy him until the end of
the war. While it may be argued that not all of the works treated
on the following pages are explicitly concerned with the Third
Reich, they all owe their existence to a burning hatred of fascism
and war, whether they deal directly with Hitler's Germany or
Franco's Spain, or indirectly with the impact of fascism in
the fictitious Land of Yahoo or the ancient Rome of Lucullus.
Since the job of Marxist teacher yielded to that of actively fighting Hitler, it seems only logical to consider Brecht's anti-Nazi
writings in a separate chapter.

I Die Rundköpfe und die Spitzköpfe
(Roundheads and Peakheads)

In 1931 Brecht accepted a commission from a Berlin stage
director to adapt Shakespeare's *Measure for Measure*. It is
obvious that the problem of class justice provoked the newly
confirmed Marxist and, in keeping with his simultaneously expanding notions of a new epic theater, he superimposed on the
original dramatic plot narrative elements from Heinrich von
Kleist's novella *Michael Kohlhas*, known to every German and
also dealing with justice. At the time of Hitler's coming to power,
the third draft of the new work was about to be published, but
the Nazis confiscated the galleys. Brecht continued to rewrite
the play in his Danish exile and the German version, now to
be found in his *Collected Works*, was first published in London
in 1938. It substantially follows the text of the first production,
which took place in Copenhagen in 1936. Curiously, however,
two English translations had already appeared in Moscow (in
1935 and 1937) before the German original became accessible.
Few Brecht plays underwent as many changes as *Die Rundköpfe
und die Spitzköpfe* (Roundheads and Peakheads), including
at least four different titles, and it may be the clouds surrounding
the writing and publication of an ever-changing script that
made most critics shy away from discussing it adequately. Only
the East-German scholar Werner Mittenzwei, who claims to
have seen all pertinent materials in the Brecht Archives, has
given a thorough, though biased, account.[2]

All available evidence suggests that Brecht was not originally concerned with the theme of racial prejudice, and even less concerned with the specific problem of anti-semitism. Neither did he wish to write an anti-Hitler play. He wanted to present a commentary on the manipulation of law and justice by class and wealth according to Marx. While he was endeavoring to fuse two literary models which seemed especially suitable to his purpose (*Measure for Measure* and *Michael Kohlhas*) into a dramatic parable on class justice, his emphasis shifted under the impact of the events he witnessed between 1932 and 1934. The result was a play as obfuscating as the period observed and as infuriating as any "light" treatment of anti-semitism must appear to post-Auschwitz audiences. The effect is somewhat similar to that of Chaplin's *The Great Dictator* whose maker neither could nor would have made his film of 1941 had he possessed full knowledge of Hitler's extermination camps. In the center of Brecht's involved double plot stands the tenant farmer Callas, who hopes to gain a team of horses from the landlord de Guzman as restitution for his daughter Nanna's seduction. Threatened by an uprising of "the Sickle League," the Viceroy of Yahoo has temporarily handed over power to Angelo Iberin, whose substitution of racial doctrines for the realities of economic inequities seems to guarantee the preservation of the status quo. Although the rich Peakhead de Guzman is sentenced to death for violating the honor of a Roundhead girl, the laws of property remain unchanged. Isabella de Guzman, a novice in a convent, is willing to save her brother by spending the night with the commandant of the prison, but Nanna Callas is finally bribed to take her place, and her father is willing to pose as the accused seducer of his daughter in order to get his rent reduced. In the end, the Viceroy returns and forces Iberin to release the landlord, while the condemned members of "the Sickle League" are waiting to be hanged. The rich, whether Roundheads or Peakheads, are united again, and Iberin prepares an attack against the neighboring land of the Squareheads.

It is easy to recognize in Brecht's fable certain parallels with German history of the Weimar period. The Viceroy is, of course, the old president and ex-general von Hindenburg, the members of "the Sickle League" are the communists, and Iberin is the drummer Hitler whom the German industrialists hoped to use as a tool against bolshevism. It is less easy to reconcile Brecht's farcical depiction of the Peakheads with the tragic fate of the Jews and it is for this reason that most critics have heaped scorn and abuse on the German playwright. It should be borne in mind, however, that in the early days of the Nazi regime many people saw in Hitler a transitory phenomenon that would not last and considered his anti-semitism primarily a tactical device for striking at a convenient and helpless scapegoat. Moreover, Brecht's failure to grasp the metaphysical nature of racism (and other aggressive drives of the human animal) is the consistent and inevitable result of his firm belief in Marxist philosophy, which makes no allowance for irrational forces incapable of economic solution. It is, therefore, not surprising that Brecht stubbornly insisted as late as 1955 that he had "in some ways" been right in his presentation of racism despite the subsequent horror of Hitler's unspeakable extermination policy; but he added that the parable is, of necessity, simplistic, although "much more clever than all other forms."[3] Since communist critics cannot concede that their theory may be wrong or, at least, incomplete, and that it has failed in the face of forces such as nationalism and racism, Werner Mittenzwei takes recourse to a lot of twisted thinking by maintaining, for instance, that Brecht had grasped the class root of fascist racism in his play. On the other hand, Frederic Ewen is equally wrong when he states: "Now, in his Danish exile, he [Brecht] began to revise it [*Die Rundköpfe und die Spitzköpfe*] in view of the gruesome changes that had taken place: the Reichstag Fire and the Nuremberg racial laws, which had also deepened his own understanding of the nature of fascism."[4] In the first place, there is no trace of the Reichstag Fire in Brecht's satirical parable; and, in the second place, the Nuremberg racial laws were not promulgated until 1935, when Brecht had substantially completed his play.

It is not surprising that *Die Rundköpfe und die Spitzköpfe* has hardly been performed since its opening in 1936 and has remained one of Brecht's least known works. The play is equally painful to communist and Western sensibilities in view of recent world history, because the circumstances of the plot make an identification of Brecht's Peakheads with the victims of Auschwitz inevitable. Moreover, the figure of Iberin is ambiguous and artistically unsatisfying. In the first drafts, he had been an honest and almost tragic character betrayed by the ruling property class. Brecht obviously tried to change him into a cynical opportunist, but he did not succeed in making him convincing and three-dimensional and, even if he had succeeded, the historical fact of Hitler's anti-semitic terror would make the responses of readers or audiences still more bitter today. On the other hand, one should not overlook the fact that Iberin is not the central character. Callas, his daughter Nanna, and the brothel-keeper, Madame Cornamontis dominate the most effective scenes; and the two ladies especially have the most humorous lines in the play and sing some of the best songs Brecht ever wrote. As a satire on the petit bourgeois origin of Hitler and the link between fascism and property rights, *Die Rundköpfe und die Spitzköpfe* succeeds; as a parable about the origin of racism, it is a failure, due to the philosophical limitations of Marxism.

II Furcht und Elend des Dritten Reiches
(The Private Life of the Master Race)

In his Danish exile, Brecht tried to maintain as close a contact with his native country as circumstances would permit. He cut out newspaper clippings and pasted them in scrapbooks; he monitored radio broadcasts, talked with escaped refugees, and incessantly discussed Germany with his friends and visitors. The major dramatic result of this concern for a documented picture of Nazi Germany was a sequence of some thirty sketches written between 1934 and 1938. It is apparent that Brecht did not originally aim at writing a play in any sense of the word, but he later provided a frame through introductory and connecting poems and, still later, through a very effective scenic device: an armored tank whose crew symbolizes the murderous extreme to which the civilian life depicted in *Furcht und Elend des Dritten Reiches* (Terror and Misery in the Third Reich) must inevitably lead. Americans know a shortened version of seventeen scenes which Eric Bentley translated under the felicitous title of *The Private Life of the Master Race* in 1944. While the longest version (twenty-seven scenes), published in London in 1938, is extinct, the "official" German edition now contains twenty-four scenes. Stage performances, mostly in abridged form, have been frequent and have occurred in many countries ever since the first production of eight scenes in Paris under the title 99% in 1938.

Brecht's chronicle of life under the Nazis spans the first five years of the Third Reich, from Hitler's becoming chancellor on January 30, 1933, until his march into Austria on March 13, 1938. The scenes vary in length from tiny vignettes (ten lines) to short, self-contained one-act plays. Since Brecht aimed at conveying the fear and misery of the average anonymous person during the Nazi period, he introduced no historical or prominent characters. We meet workers, storm troopers, maids, bakers, teachers, judges, scientists, doctors, farmers, butchers, storekeepers, clergymen, soldiers, schoolboys—in short, a cross section of the population. As usual, the author reserves his deadliest scorn for the intellectuals, whom he justly scolds for meek submission in the face of better judgment. Although Brecht's aim was political, he refrained from the exaggerations of mere propaganda, and the result of his semidocumentary style is a truthful account of life under the Nazis, which, despite its many gruesome aspects, does not lack a certain mixture of touching pathos and sardonic humor. As an eyewitness who lived through these five years in Germany, I can testify to the accuracy of a picture which the exiled author succeeded in creating with an uncanny feeling for correct detail despite his physical remoteness from the described events. If I have one criticism nevertheless, it is the fact that a certain residue of wishful thinking led Brecht to convey to the uninformed outsider (and he wrote these scenes for outsiders!) the false impression that life under Hitler was fear and misery to *all* Germans. Today we must say: this was, unfortunately, not the case; if it had been, the Third Reich would not have lasted as long as it did.

"The Jewish Wife" is probably the most famous and the most durable of Brecht's "miniatures of monstrosity," as Bentley has aptly called them. The Jewish-born wife of a non-Jewish physician has decided to emigrate to Amsterdam in order to spare her husband further harrassment and to save his position in a clinic;

with the economy of the born dramatist, Brecht has condensed a psychologically complex situation into one single scene consisting of the woman's farewell telephone calls to a few acquaintances, her rehearsal of the speech intended to inform her husband, and the final confrontation of the couple. Often performed, filmed as well as produced for television, the little play continues to serve as a vehicle for leading actresses. Two other sketches, while less dramatic, also survive as theater pieces: "In Search of Justice" shows the pitiful plight of a judge who is about to try a case according to the often quoted notorious pronouncement by the Nazi Minister of Justice: "Whatever is useful to the German nation is just." "The Informer" portrays a typical domestic scene of Nazi family life: distrust and fear of denunciation on the part of a high school teacher and his wife in the presence of their young son. It is amazing how accurately Brecht reproduced the peculiar vernacular of the Third Reich, although by then he had to work from memory and on the basis of newspaper clippings. While not likely to be performed outside of Germany in the future, *Furcht und Elend des Dritten Reiches* will continue to be of considerable interest to the cultural historian.

III Frau Carrars Gewehre
(Señora Carrar's Rifles)

When, in 1936, the Spanish Army chiefs rebelled against the newly established Republic of Spain founded five years earlier, the sympathies of most of the civilized world belonged to the Republican forces. That a man like Brecht could not remain indifferent to the struggle was to be expected, especially since Franco was aided by Hitler and Mussolini and the Loyalists were eventually dominated and led by the Communists. In 1937, before the outcome was decided, Brecht contributed a short play, which was given a stirring production with Helene Weigel in the same year in Paris and has since become his most frequently performed play in East Germany. *Frau Carrars Gewehre* (Señora Carrar's Rifles) is an updated, politicized version of John Millington Synge's famous one-act drama *Riders to the Sea* (1904). Teresa Carrar, who has lost her Andalusian fisherman husband in the civil war, is determined to keep her two sons out of the fighting. Things come to a climax when her brother asks her to hand over a cache of rifles still hidden in the house. Supported only by the local priest, who also believes in neutrality, Teresa remains steadfast in her refusal, until the neighbors silently carry in the body of Juan, her oldest son, who had been out fishing when he was killed by a Nationalist gunboat. Now Teresa not only turns over the rifles but leaves for the front herself.

I have already pointed out the ironical fact that Brecht achieved his greatest popular success with his least original major play, *Die Dreigroschenoper*. A similar observation may be in order concerning Brecht's appreciation in his own political camp. The record shows that there were fifty-four separate productions of *Frau Carrars Gewehre* in various cities of the German Democratic Republic between 1947 and 1967, more than twice as many as of any other Brecht play; there have also been frequent performances in other communist countries. The answer is simple: it is the only play which is traditional in terms of nonepic dramatic structure, climax, straight prose dialogue, and the absence of any deliberate attempt at stylization. In short, it conforms to the concept of "socialist realism" and is free of "formalism." It speaks for the artist Brecht that he was not fooled by the approval his play received from Party critics. In a note, attached to the 1954 edition of his collected plays, he apologetically mentions the Aristotelian dramaturgy of "this little play" and points at "the disadvantages of this technique." What some of his Marxist critics praised as progress and as a sign of maturity was to him a regrettable regression, only justified as a spontaneous contribution to the immediate fight against fascism but leading to a temporary neglect of his dramatic theories.

There is no denying that "the little play" is effective. Any reasonably good actress is bound to make Teresa Carrar deeply moving. On the other hand, there is also a certain crudeness and simplistic psychology about a dramatic piece in which the leading character diametrically shifts positions within a few minutes, not out of any deep insight but emotionally motivated by a mixture of grief and rage. By denying himself the richer

devices of his epic theater for adequately showing the complexities of both the civil war and his main character, Brecht
subordinated his potentially greater gifts as a literary artist
to the temporary goal of a political activist trying to stop fascism.

IV   Das Verhör des Lukullus
(The Trial of Lucullus)

In 1940, Radio Berne (Switzerland) produced a short play
Brecht had written a year earlier. Composed in the new irregular
free verse of *Heilige Johanna* with only one rhymed speech,
the brief dramatic poem may perhaps best be called a cantata
and is far removed in style and spirit from the realism of the
last two works we have just considered. Since it was, however,
undoubtedly inspired by Brecht's increased hatred of war
following the Munich crisis of 1938, and in the face of almost
certain further imminent exploits by Hitler, it seems reasonable
to deal with the play in the context of this chapter. It is easy
to see that Imperial Rome, with its warlike heroism, would seem
to offer a pertinent parallel to Nazi Germany; a reminder of
the transitoriness of pure conquest in the eyes of posterity,
although not likely to stop a Hitler, might well be worth the
attention of all those who were still capable of rational thought.

General Lucullus has died. His pompous funeral procession,
including slaves carrying the triumphal frieze for his monument,
is stopped at the burial place. A jury consisting of a peasant,
a slave, a fishwife, a baker, and a courtesan is about to decide
whether the great warrior should be admitted to the Elysian
Fields or condemned to extinction in the underworld. Unaided,
Lucullus has to defend himself. When he calls Alexander the
Great as his star witness, most expert to testify to his conquests,
he is told that there is no Alexander of Macedon in the Elysian
Fields. Now the figures of his frieze are called upon to speak.
Only the cook is not entirely negative in his statement because
Lucullus showed a "human" interest in food and gave his culinary
artistry free range. Ultimately, however, it is the import of the
cherry tree from Asia, praised by the peasant juror, that un-
qualifiedly speaks for Lucullus. Since the announced criterion is
usefulness, the question now before the judge and the jury is:

does a deed which could have been accomplished with the services of the one man who carried the tree justify the death of eighty thousand slain soldiers?

In the original radio play, the jury withdraws after Scene XIII to deliberate on the verdict. The audience, so to speak, would pass the answer. A great deal of abuse has been heaped upon Brecht by his debunkers because he added a fourteenth scene in 1951 when an operatic production in Berlin (music by Paul Dessau) caused a rift with the East German authorities. He also gave a few additional lines to the frieze figure of a king defeated by Lucullus who now boasts that he organized a (futile) defense against Rome. A calm examination of the text and the circumstances surrounding the revision must exonerate Brecht, in my opinion. In the first place, the thrust of the cantata has remained unchanged; there can be no doubt as to the verdict, even without hearing it pronounced by the jury. Most criticism stems from the fact that Brecht changed the title of the opera to *Die Verurteilung des Lukullus* (The Condemnation of Lucullus) under pressure. However, he not only gave permission to produce and print the first version in the West, but himself retained the original title *Das Verhör des Lukullus* (The Trial of Lucullus) in the edition of his plays which he published in 1954, together with explicit notes listing the revisions in the opera. Nineteen fifty-one, when the clash with the Ulbricht regime occurred, was the time of the Korean War, and the question of defensive wars versus aggressive wars was very much alive. When Brecht wrote the play, he obviously had Hitler's imminent war in mind, but he certainly did not condemn the subsequent Allied defense operations.

It seems to me that the Vietnam War has lately provided many persons, especially Americans, with a new perspective for judging Brecht more objectively for what he did with his opera in 1951. An essentially antimilitaristic and pacifistic writer since his earliest beginnings, he made a few tactical, and decisively minor, changes in order to have his opera shown rather than withdrawn. In a somewhat reverse dilemma of a similar moral dimension, many conscientious objectors have recently found themselves in the position of rejecting all wars to escape service in Vietnam rather than approving only certain wars, such as that against Hitler. Is an author who saves a basically pacifistic script by inserting a few lines in favor of defensive war more reprehensible than the objector to a specific immoral war who resorts to a white lie because an inadequate law forces him to pose as an all-out pacifist? Even Esslin, who is otherwise very critical of Brecht's political compromises, concedes that "he did not make any really important changes, certainly none that altered the character of the work as a whole."[5] Moreover, there is evidence that the official furor against the opera was also due, in large measure, to Paul Dessau's "formalistic" music. As to the enforced change of title, it only made explicit what the "trial" of the original version had already clearly implied. As always, Brecht enjoyed the controversy with the functionaries of the Ministry of Culture immensely and is said to have remarked, with his customary tongue-in-cheek: "Where else in the world can you find a government that shows such interest in, and pays such attention to, artists?"

V Der aufhaltsame Aufstieg des Arturo Ui (The Resistible Rise of Arturo Ui)

While waiting for his American visa in Helsinki, Brecht started, and finished within a few weeks in the spring of 1941, a "gangster" play he had first conceived during his earlier visit to New York on the occasion of the performance of *The Mother* in 1935. Most Brecht scholars claim that the German playwright aimed at explaining Hitler's ascent to Americans in their own terms of reference and hoped to get a play, set in Chicago, the battleground of the notorious Al Capone, produced more easily. If this is true, it only shows how naïve and tactless Brecht could be at times. Was it likely that audiences in his new host country would be thrilled by a "gangster spectacle" (Brecht's own words) in which the warmongering and universally hated Führer at the height of his military conquests was reduced to a small-scale racketeer and killer? Might they not rather resent factual distortions of the Chicago scene due to the forced parallel to Nazi Germany? When he reached America a few weeks later, Brecht must have sensed how unsuitable his new script was under the circumstances, and he apparently made no serious effort to have it produced. America's entry into the war in December of the same year and the subsequent climate of genuine patriotism finally ruled out any performance for the time being. It is interesting that Brecht left the original version untouched during his later years with the Berlin Ensemble, in contrast to other plays he revised and produced before his death. It was not until 1958 that the first performance took place in Stuttgart, with only mild success, and it was not until 1960 that a brilliant touring production of the Berlin Ensemble in Paris attracted worldwide attention. The American adaptation on the New York stage in the late sixties met with decidedly mixed reactions.

Brecht's Adolf Hitler is a minor gangster named Arturo Ui who worms his way into the Cauliflower Trust of Chicago, whose wholesalers he wishes to "protect." In his endeavor, he blackmails the corrupt mayor Dogsborough, liquidates one of his own rebellious henchmen, Ernesto Roma, and murders Ignatius Dullfeet, a businessman in the neighboring town of Cicero, whose newspaper had criticized the terror of Ui's gang. At the end, the greengrocers of Cicero, led by Dullfeet's widow Betty, join the Chicago trust and ask for Ui's protection. Anybody familiar with the Nazi record will easily recognize the allusions to German history during Hitler's ascent up to the annexation of Austria. Mayor Dogsborough is, of course, President von Hindenburg, whom the big East-Prussian landowners converted into an "interested party" by presenting him with an estate once owned by his ancestors. The burning of the German Reichstag by the Nazis reappears as a Chicago warehouse fire with a subsequent show trial in which the alleged arsonist remains incoherent under the influence of drugs. When Ernesto Roma, the most loyal of Ui's henchmen, is killed, we are reminded of the bloody purge of June 30, 1934, during which Hitler's closest friend, Ernst Röhm, the leader of the Brown Shirts (SA) was liquidated. In Dullfeet of Cicero we recognize Austria's semidictatorial chancellor Dollfuss, who was assassinated by the Nazis in 1934 and whose country was taken over by the "protector" Hitler in 1938. Quite apart from these broader allusions and obvious parallels, there are innumerable references to biographical and psychological facts which an American audience in 1941 could not have fully appreciated but which were relished by postwar theatergoers who had, in the meantime, become familiar with the leading Nazi hoodlums. One of the funniest, psychologically most penetrating (and historically true) episodes, for instance, occurs in the seventh scene when Ui takes private lessons in public speaking and posture from an old ham actor and recites Anthony's famous oration with the repeated line "but Brutus is an honorable man."

Brecht was aware of the danger of cheap travesty which might reduce Hitler to a silly clown, and therefore chose the form of a Shakespearean historical spectacle and insisted that it be staged "in the grand manner," as he stated in a few remarks following the original printed text. It is, however, doubtful whether he succeeded in his aim, despite the use of blank verse and the imitation of Shakespeare. The Marxist knew that the bourgeois mentality tends to romanticize criminals, and he hoped that the "estrangement effect" of transposing a contemporary historical figure like Hitler into the alien environment of a quasi-legendary setting would induce an audience to focus more objectively. He wrote: "The great political criminals must be exposed, more than anything else, to ridicule, because they are not so much *great* political criminals as perpetrators of great political crimes—which is not the same thing."[6] At heart there is the problem of the "banality of evil," which Hannah Arendt demonstrated when she reported on the Eichmann trial in Jerusalem. She convincingly showed that a mass murderer can be a petit bourgeois bureaucrat at heart rather than a monster a la Gilles de Rais. However, the case of Hitler is more complex, and it seems to me that the satanic ingredients of his character are as little susceptible to Marxist interpretation as they are to parabolic presentation. Charlie Chaplin was more successful in solving the same artistic problem with his highly stylized *Great Dictator* of the same year, although it is very doubtful that, as I have stated before, he would have attempted his satire with the full knowledge of Auschwitz a few years later. The brilliance of the Berlin Ensemble production could deceive audiences into overrating a play which, despite undeniable flashes of genius, must be judged a failure resulting from Brecht's lapse of good judgment.

VI   Die Gesichte der Simone Machard
(The Visions of Simone Machard)

American exile did not only reunite Brecht with his old mentor of the early Munich days, Lion Feuchtwanger, but it led to the second active collaboration of the two men since *Eduard der Zweite* (Edward the Second). Moved by Feuchtwanger's reminiscences of the collapse of France that included confinement in a French internment camp and flight from the advancing Germans, Brecht started work on a play which he had already planned in Finland, *Jeanne D'Arc 1940*, his second variation on the theme of Saint Joan. After several scenes had been quickly completed and Feuchtwanger had already started to write his novel *Simone*, the two writers finally started to collaborate (from the fall of 1942 to early 1943) on the play which was then called *Heilige Johanna von Vitry* (Saint Joan of Vitry) and ultimately received the title of *Die Gesichte der Simone Machard* (The Visions of Simone Machard). It was not until after Brecht's death that the first performance took place in Frankfurt in 1957.

This time, the new saint is an adolescent peasant girl, the setting is a little country hotel in the middle of France, and the time is June, 1940, during the German breakthrough. Simone works for Mr. Soupeau, whose business includes a gasoline station and two trucks and who, together with his old Pétainist mother, is about to save his own supplies and to transport the wines of Captain Fétain, a French fascist, despite the pleas of the mayor of the little town. The naïve and uneducated girl, whose seventeen-year-old brother André serves in the army as a volunteer, becomes infatuated with a book about Saint Joan that the patron has given her with the sanctimonious words: "The Lord knows we could use a Maid of Orleans." Inspired by several visions in which André appears as an angel, Mr. Soupeau as the Connétable, his mother as Queen Isabel, the mayor as King Charles VII, and Captain Fétain as the Duke of Burgundy, Simone sees herself as Jeanne and defies her employers. She feeds the starving refugees and sets fire to the hoarded gasoline before it can be handed over to the occupying Germans. In her subsequent last vision, Simone is tried and sentenced to death, but in reality the Germans hand her over to the French, since she is only a minor and the truce Marshal

Pétain has in the meantime concluded is now in force. She is being led away by two nuns to an institution for the feebleminded to which she will be committed.

Most professional Brechtians are embarrassed by this play, which strikes them as sentimental and simplistic. To compound the offense, it is also neither Marxist nor epic. I am not denying the fact that Brecht has created more complex and memorable characters and a richer linguistic texture elsewhere, but in purely theatrical terms the play is undoubtedly moving and effective. The four acts, each alternating between the real world of 1940 and Simone's dream visions, move swiftly; the characters, although more or less stereotypes, are well contrasted and chosen with admirable economy; there is a lot of visually interesting stage business and even a modest amount of suspense. As is so often true in cases of publicly acknowledged collaboration, it is difficult to know precisely who did what. Feuchtwanger's own experiences and his subsequent novel undoubtedly provided the impetus for the whole venture. It is also probable that the internationally known novelist and Hollywood-attuned author of 1942, who was admittedly bored by Brecht's theories, exerted his moderating influence on the relatively brief and straight-forward script. On the other hand, we now know that Brecht had originally planned the play in Finland two years earlier and had already sketched several scenes in 1941 before reading his friend's novel *Simone*. And what could be a more Brechtian touch than the very end of the play, when a second burning building is observed with the comment "It seems the refugees learned something! Simone will be able to see it on her way to the institution!" There is an even more convincing reason for Brecht's suspension of non-Aristotelian technique in this play: the immediacy of the provocation and his polemic intent. Just as the intensely felt reality of the Third Reich provoked the simple sketches of *Furcht und Elend des Dritten Reiches,* and the Spanish civil war the realistic one-acter *Frau Carrars Gewehre,* so the deeply resented collapse of France at the height of Hitler's victories was bound to lead to a plea for resistance in the disguise of a fast-moving play free of the usual complexities. In view of the great popularity of *Frau Carrars Gewehre,* it is entirely conceivable that renewed interest in the

France of Pétain—evidenced by documentary films such as *The Sorrow and the Pity*—may also result in a new evaluation of Brecht's *Die Gesichte der Simone Machard.*

VII   Schweyk im Zweiten Weltkrieg
(Schweyk in the Second World War)

Hollywood, which Brecht loathed, nevertheless had some redeeming value for him because it brought him together with a number of illustrious fellow refugees from pre-Hitler Berlin. Now the gregarious playwright, who had always been most productive when surrounded by friends, and who was a compulsive debater, could once more enjoy the kind of stimulating company that was denied him during the relatively lonely years of Scandinavian exile. While Brecht tried to make a living as a screen writer and adapter of stage vehicles for stars such as Elisabeth Bergner (mostly without success), he managed to pursue his own literary work, including poetry as well as prose, at an amazing pace. With the war in Europe raging more furiously than ever and a Nazi victory still a sinister possibility, Brecht continued to devote most of his energies to fighting Hitler with his pen. One of the finest results of this polemic writing is a play, *Schweyk im Zweiten Weltkrieg* (Schweyk in the Second World War), almost totally unknown in America, not yet available in a published English translation, and generally not adequately treated by most Brecht scholars.

One of the highlights of Berlin's 1928 theatrical season was Erwin Piscator's production of *The Good Soldier Schweik*, a dramatization of Jaroslav Hašek's satire on the stupidity of Imperial Austria's bureaucracy and military machinery. In the center of the rambling novel is the Prague dogcatcher Schweik, who is drafted as punishment for a supposed insult to the Emperor, lands in an Austrian prisoner of war camp in a Russian uniform and, finally, finds himself as a Russian prisoner in the midst of the Russian revolution. Hašek, who himself defected to the Russians, died in 1923 and never completed the novel; but what he left behind was published as a book and won international acclaim. Schweik, who has been dubbed a Czech Sancho Panza by some critics, is the epitome of the little man who survives by a combination of being stupid and playing dumb and by cheerfully adjusting to every situation however implausible or dangerous. Piscator, who saw the possibilities inherent in the material for his Agit-Prop theater, rejected a dramatization submitted to him by two authors, one of whom was Kafka's old friend Max Brod; he commissioned three new writers, among them Brecht. Now, fifteen years later, conversations with the actor Oskar Homolka, an old friend, brought back memories of the glorious Piscator production; there was added the desire to create a suitable role for Peter Lorre, who had starred in several early Brecht plays; and after Kurt Weill, who had become a popular Broadway composer in the meantime, agreed to contribute the music, Brecht set out to change the old Schweik into a new *Schweyk im Zweiten Weltkrieg*. However, Weill withdrew when American friends advised him of the unsuitability of the script for the commercial theater. It was not until the year before his death that Brecht was thinking of a production with his own Berlin Ensemble, and though he still heard Hanns Eisler play the newly composed score for him, the play remained unpublished and unproduced during his lifetime. The world premiere took place in Warsaw in 1957, followed by subsequent productions in many European countries, including both Germanys, France, and Italy.

The new Schweyk is a dog-dealer, this time in German-occupied Prague, and he still meets his friends in a tavern, "The Goblet," now run by Mrs. Kopecka, a staunchly nationalistic and handsome widow pursued by a young Czech butcher and a German Gestapo agent. Inasmuch as there is a central plot, it revolves around Schweyk's theft of a dog, owned by a Czech Quisling but wanted by an SS bully for his wife. There is also Schweyk's gluttonous friend Baloun, tempted to enlist in the German army for the sake of ampler rations but restrained by his Czech friends. Schweyk's ambiguous words and actions involve him in a series of screamingly funny but hair-raisingly dangerous adventures and situations, such as an interrogation in the Gestapo headquarters, a stint in the Voluntary Labor Service, confinement in a military prison among fellow Czech malingerers, and finally induction into the German army at the Russian front. The eight scenes of action are preceded by

a prologue and two interludes in "the Higher Regions," in which
a monster-sized Hitler is reassured of the love of "the common
man" for him by an equally monster-sized Goering and Himmler
and a dwarf-sized Goebbels. In the epilogue, Schweyk, lost in
a snowstorm fifty kilometers from Stalingrad and trying to
regain his regiment, confronts a bewildered Hitler, who is also
lost because his path is blocked in all directions: in the north
by the snow, in the south by frozen corpses, in the east by
the Red Army, and in the west by the German people he does
not dare face. After Hitler, whose futile goose-stepping finally
turns into a grotesque dance, has disappeared in the snow,
the whole cast steps to the ramp of the stage and triumphantly
repeats "The Moldau Song," which Mrs. Kopecka had already
sung earlier and which ends the play on a note of change
and hope:

> Es wechseln die Zeiten. Die riesigen Pläne
> Der Mächtigen kommen am Ende zum Halt.
> Und gehn sie einher auch wie blutige Hähne
> Es wechseln die Zeiten, da hilft kein Gewalt.
>
> Am Grunde der Moldau wandern die Steine.
> Es liegen drei Kaiser begraben in Prag.
> Das Grosse bleibt gross nicht und klein nicht das Kleine.
> Die Nacht hat zwölf Stunden, dann kommt schon der Tag.
>
> (The times will be changing. The intricate plotting
> Of people in power must finally fail.
> Like bloodthirsty cocks though today they are strutting
> The times will be changing, force cannot prevail.
>
> The stones on the Moldau's bottom go shifting
> In Prague three emperors molder away.
> The top won't stay top, for the bottom is lifting
> The night has twelve hours and is followed by day.)[7]

When Martin Esslin somewhat condescendingly states that
Brecht's play is a pastiche of "Hašek's language and characteriza-
tion," he is not correct. It would be more accurate to say that
Brecht, after having reread the novel during a train ride from

New York to Hollywood in 1943, nevertheless used the Berlin dramatization (probably from memory) as the basis for a new play that had already been on his mind a year earlier. While it is true that he lifted many scenes from the German translation of the novel almost verbatim, he nevertheless confined himself to the episodes of the Piscator adaptation on which he had worked before. He tightened the dramatic structure by reducing the number of characters and placing the tavern ("The Goblet") as a unifying locus in the center of his new play. Most important, however, he changed Hašek's (and Piscator's) imbecile and involuntarily hilarious Schweik into a slightly less stupid and egocentric and somewhat more "human" Schweyk, still a rascal, but one with empathy and even the willingness to help others at some risk to himself. At the same time, Brecht was careful to make his hero neither too good nor too cunning, and noted: "Under no circumstances must Schweyk be conceived as a sly, underhanded saboteur. He is simply the opportunist of the few opportunities offered him."[8] In other words, it is chiefly his indestructibility which fascinated Brecht and which he always considered the main strength of the people and the first prerequisite for liberation. When the playwright appeared a few years later before the House Committee on Un-American Activities, he must have taken Schweyk as his model, and some of his most memorable stage characters, such as Galileo, Shen-Te, Grusha, and Azdak (see the next chapter), are similarly motivated by "enlightened self-interest."

Schweyk, the little man, is bent on surviving; he is no hero of the resistance, but if his kind of cheerful compliance were multiplied a thousand times, it would be tantamount to sabotage. Neither is he an outright collaborationist; he even tries to prevent his friend Baloun from becoming one. When he finds himself separated from his unit near Stalingrad, he sets out to rejoin it because he would otherwise risk either freezing and starving to death or being killed by Russian partisans; but the play leaves no doubt that the winning odds for an army of Schweyks are not exactly great. In 1927, when Brecht worked on the Piscator adaptation, he had already told a friend how he planned to incorporate this notion. He imagined a scene in which General Ludendorff, standing before gigantic maps in a room two stories high, would be seen directing the movements of vast armies that never arrived at the right time, or the right place, or in the right numerical strength, while in a cellar underneath many soldiers are shown, all of them looking like Schweyk. Brecht commented: "They follow all instructions, they respect their superiors, they move when ordered; but they never arrive at their destination in time, and never in their full complement."[9] In addition to confirming Brecht's notion of resistance by compliance, the comment also illustrates what we have had repeated occasion to observe: his ability to use and rework old ideas and scenic images after long periods of dormancy. Thus, Ludendorff in the giant room became the larger-than-life Hitler in "the Higher Regions" and in the snowstorm. Finally, there may be one more reason why Schweyk did not become a more active resistance fighter like Simone. Brecht always retained a slightly romanticized notion of the German people under the Nazis, and in 1943 he was actively engaged in appeals to prominent refugees as well as to the general public concerning the future of Germany. He still saw Germany as a country of millions of Schweyks trying to survive under the heel of a few brutes and bullies. What he failed to realize is the sad fact that the Schweyks, and the Brechts who love them, have neither been numerous in Germany nor typical of the German people. However, what his play may have lacked as an effective anti-Hitler propaganda piece in 1943, it has since gained as a satirical comedy, almost timeless by now, tightly structured, rich in folksy wisdom, hilarious in situations and characterization, and poetically enhanced by some of the finest songs Brecht ever wrote.

CHAPTER 5

The Master Plays
or the Redemption of Exile

AN artist who enters the fourth decade of his life is generally assumed to have reached the peak of his maturity and creative powers. Brecht is no exception, despite his extraordinarily precocious talent, which had already enabled him to enrich the modern poetic idiom of Germany at the age of eighteen, and to endow the theater with plays as enduring as *Die Dreigroschenoper*, to write one of the most relevant modern tragedies, *Die Massnahme*, and to create one of the finest examples of twentieth century poetic drama, *Die heilige Johanna der Schlachthöfe*, when he was barely thirty years old. If as yet there is no general agreement among the critics and the public about some of these works because they are rarely performed, there is a consensus that Brecht wrote his theatrical masterpieces in his forties—i.e., between 1938 and 1945. This is as it should be, except that, in his case, we must consider exile as a factor added to the normal process of aging and maturing. Ordinarily exile is not a salutary experience, because it imposes economic and physical deprivations on a writer, let alone emotional problems and spiritual wounds caused by an often hostile and, at best, alien environment. There are numerous tragic examples among Brecht's fellow refugees who succumbed to despair and, finally, even committed suicide. While I do not wish to belittle the hardships Brecht suffered from being denied the stages of his native country and forced to move from one foreign country whose language he hardly or not at all understood to another, it seems to me that exile proved to be beneficial to him in at least two ways. First, it interrupted and modified a life-style that was too hectic even for him and detrimental to measured thought and quiet contemplation. Already in the 1920's in Berlin,

the playwright had complained that the daily hustle and bustle
of the theater made serious sustained work impossible, and he
had made a practice of escaping to Augsburg during the sum-
mers in order to write. Now, being cut off from the use of a
live stage and no longer surrounded by a swarm of admirers
and co-workers, Brecht found himself with more time to write,
think, and read. Second, the inevitable exigencies of exile
brought about a certain measure of separation from Berlin Party
functionaries and policy arguments, followed by growing disenchantment with "socialist realism" as he had occasion to observe it, and culminating in his shock over the Stalin-Ribbentrop
pact of 1939. Thus, the mellowing of Brecht's previous didacticism was undoubtedly helped along by the new and wider
perspectives he attained through personal experiences in exile.

We have already remarked that Brecht's dramatic theories
developed simultaneously with his study of Marxism. We should,
therefore, expect that the aesthetics of the newly converted
Marxist became less rigid as his ethos, although still basically
intact, was modified by the influence of intellectual friends
during many discussions and through reading of their books in
exile. As Brecht's revulsion against the narrow definition of
Party-approved realism increased, he tended more and more
toward the long and complex Shakespearean chronicle play and
the timeless parable as models for his dramatic writing. There
may be still another reason why his most acclaimed masterpieces
represent these two types of drama less restricted by actually
experienced reality. We observed in Chapter 1 that Brecht's
imagination located some of his earlier works in a fictitious
America, which ceased to interest him once he had set foot in the
real United States, and that he was either unwilling or unable
to accommodate the Ulbricht regime with a play about the
realities of the GDR. He apparently felt that the distance imposed by history and parabolic presentation was more conducive
to his broadening aesthetic concepts, which required artistic
stylization to the highest possible degree. If one studies the
international list of persons with whom Brecht had intellectual
intercourse in various countries, and the many books he read
in those years, the conclusion seems justified that the hardships
of his exile were redeemed by a few great plays indebted to it.

I   Mutter Courage und ihre Kinder
(Mother Courage and Her Children)

The subtitle, "A Chronicle of the Thirty Years' War," gives a clue to the major literary source of this play, as far as time, setting, and the name of the leading character are concerned. *The Runagate Courage* is the title of a minor novel about an adventuress called "Vagabond Courashe" by Germany's greatest Baroque novelist, Hans Jakob Christian von Grimmelshausen, whose chief picaresque work, *The Adventurous Simplicissimus*, is familiar to every German for its realistic depiction of that most terrible of all wars (1618–48).[1] The second and, probably, more direct stimulus for Brecht's play came from a Swedish actress, Naima Wifstrand, who read to him a ballad about a sutler woman, Lotta Svärd, from J. L. Runeberg's *Songs of Ensign Stal*, and for whom Brecht, who then resided in Lidingö near Stockholm, intended to write a part. The third provocation seems obvious. World War II had broken out on September 1, 1939, and had been raging for four weeks when Brecht started writing on September 27. The play was finished by November, but no Swedish production materialized. The world premiere in the original German took place in Zurich in 1941, without Brecht being able to attend. His own, slightly changed Berlin production of 1949 provided Helene Weigel with the most celebrated role of her career and culminated in touring triumphs for the Berlin Ensemble in Paris (1954) and London (1956). As usual, Brecht did not fare as well on the stages of the United States as on those of most other countries, and a mediocre New York production in the 1960's failed to do justice to his play. This is all the more regrettable, since a strong interest in it is manifest and may be deduced by the fact that two published and five unpublished English translations exist.

Brecht took nothing but the nickname "Courage" and the Thirty Years' War from Grimmelshausen, whose heroine is a seductive, pleasure-loving, childless harlot of illegitimate but aristocratic birth. From Runeberg's Lotta Svärd, who accompanied the soldiers of Gustavus III in the eighteenth century, he retained only her status as a sutler woman who remained a good trooper and comfort to the troops even in old age. *Mutter Cour-*

age und ihre Kinder is an entirely original work by Brecht, both in terms of dramatic structure and in its characters. For twelve scenes (from 1624 until 1636) we follow the canteen wagon of Anna Fierling, who makes a living from the war but wishes to keep her three children out of it. Each child, by a different father, represents one virtue in excess and is consequently killed by it. Schweizerkäs (Swiss Cheese), dumb but honest, refuses to hand over the regimental cash box and is shot, although his mother could have bought him off; but she haggled too long. Courageous Eilif, her oldest son, is executed because during a short peace interlude he repeats a brutal deed for which he had been praised while the war was raging. Kattrin, her disfigured and mute daughter, is shot down by soldiers while beating a drum in order to rouse the citizens of a besieged town. Worn out, old and numb with grief, Mother Courage harnesses herself to the wagon, the only possession left to her, to catch up with the army, because, as she almost compulsively mutters, "I must go back into business."

Scholars and critics who are unsympathetic to Brecht's anti-illusionist dramatic theories never tire of gleefully pointing out that his instinctive artistry triumphed over his arid notions in this play. They cite the fact that most audiences sympathize with the heroine as a great mother figure and are touched to tears by her fate, which they consider genuinely tragic. There is no denying the fact that Anna Fierling is seen in several deeply touching and emotionally charged scenes, no matter how poor the performance may be; and even the reading of the text will elicit some such responses. Since Brecht expressly and repeatedly stated that emotions are by no means to be excluded from his epic theater (he was only against an audience's intellectual drain caused by total illusionary identification with the character on the stage), the argument against him would gain validity only if Mother Courage were a tragic character. I raised the possibility that Brecht might have written a tragedy against his will in *Die Massnahme*,[2] but I am prepared to argue that Anna Fierling, whom even one of her friends calls "a hyena of the battlefield," is and remains essentially a hard-boiled businesswoman (with a heart, of course, why not?) and is not crushed by the inevitable forces of fate. When Brecht heard of the reactions to the first Zurich performance of 1941, which caused reviewers to compare Mother Courage with the mythological mother figure of Niobe, he made a few changes to bolster the negative aspects of the character. In the original Scene V, for instance, the sutler woman was first seen withholding her supplies of linen needed for dressing the wounds of bleeding soldiers, then reluctantly yielding to pressure, and finally tearing new shirts apart in order to help. In the revised version (which has become standard for all translations and productions since 1948), Anna Fierling refuses to part with her supplies, is physically attacked by her outraged daughter, and finally forcefully dispossessed of her shirts by the chaplain; she never helps them with their Samaritan work. It is true that Brecht made his heroine into a three-dimensional character torn between her maternal instinct and her addiction to business, but her actions are never inevitable. She knows full well that war is terrible and is determined to keep her children out of it; and yet she is equally determined to make her living from it. If it did not sound too trivial, one could call her the proverbial eater of the cake she wants to keep; and this is certainly no basis for tragedy. Essentially, Mother Courage is guilty of poor judgment, and it is her business sense which prevails—sadly perhaps but not tragically—in the crucial moments of her life. Although the war is all-pervading from the first to the last scene of the play, there is no suggestion that it is ineradicable. Confronted with a simple woman of the seventeenth century during a long war which is her sustenance, we are not surprised that she curses it only once (at the end of Scene VI) and generally fears peace as a threat to her accustomed manner of making a living. Anna Fierling is a realist who adjusts to every situation and is as little capable of conscious heroism as Schweyk, whom she equals in shrewdness and the will to survive (and with whose linguistic idom Brecht endowed her). That she is herself aware of it is made clear in Scene IV when she sings "The Song of the Great Capitulation" to a young soldier who had come to voice an official complaint to the Captain (as she herself was about to do). After listening to her admonition that only a really big rage would be worth the trouble surely to be expected, and that she, too, was once capable of it, but

> Then a little bird whispered in my ear:
> "That's all very well, but wait a year
> And you will join the big brass band
> And with your trumpet in your hand
> You'll march in lockstep with the rest"

the young man storms out of the office, and she says to the clerk: "I've thought better of it. I'm not complaining." And that is why Anna Fierling does not condemn war at the end, as communist friends and critics told Brecht she should; she remains a businesswoman and does not learn. However, cannot an audience learn by watching a simple and very human person in a definite historical setting who could and possibly should, have acted and reacted differently? Brecht certainly thought so. That to him, as a Marxist, war was only the ultimate manifestation of business under capitalism, reduces Anna Fierling to a small businesswoman caught in it. Even though she might have been too ignorant and too insignificant to affect the war in any way, she did not need to stay in it as long as, and in the manner, she did. Somebody else in her circumstances might have acted quite differently. Anna Fierling's incessant haggling, which even annoys her less-than-saintly friend the Chaplain, makes her the special case of a person acting from greed and reacting from habit, rather than a tragic hero caught in the inextricable web of destiny. Her "grain of evil" is larger than most unjustifiably sympathetic interpretations on the stage reveal; a close reading of the text leaves no doubt about it. Undue sympathy for her is also caused by the length of the play, because one is bound to like a character whose every thought and action one is forced to follow for more than three hours; Brecht was furious when the perspicacious Hanns Eisler made that observation.[3] Whoever has seen Helene Weigel's "correct" performance in the filmed version of the Berlin Ensemble production will realize that Brecht has written a great and moving play, but not a tragedy.

A seeming contradiction of what I stated may be witnessed in Scene IX: the Cook, who has just inherited a little tavern in his native Utrecht, offers Mother Courage the chance to come with him and to leave her business, which, at this point, is very bad. Since he refuses to accept Kattrin because her disfigured appearance might scare away customers and the tiny inn could not support three people, Anna Fierling rejects the offer. She cannot leave her dumb and helpless daughter, who is unable to take care of herself. Niobe in action, it seems. However, some cool reflection is in order. How many mothers, given the identical circumstances, would be cruel enough to abandon a severely handicapped daughter to the certain fate of death or worse, just to obtain a modest amount of security in a momentary business depression? Such a mother would be a monster, and Anna Fierling is not a monster, as Brecht has amply shown in the eight preceding scenes. When some critics gloat over what they see as an inconsistency in the playwright's characterization, they reveal a lack of understanding of the complexities of the human psyche. It is precisely one of the achievements of the older Brecht that he was able to create memorable characters who are unique because they are full of contradictions and ambiguities. Would we, for instance, expect Mother Courage to consider the Cook's offer even for a minute while her sutler business is good (which it has been most of the time throughout the play)? Only because she is deep down in the dumps does she ponder the offer at all. To show what goes on in her mind, Brecht makes brilliant use of one of his celebrated devices, the so-called V–(estrangement) effect,[4] by having the Cook sing "The Song of the Great Souls of this Earth." In Scene IV, we have heard Mother Courage, who came to the Captain to file a complaint, singing "The Song of the Great Capitulation," seemingly to dissuade a young soldier, but in reality persuading herself to desist from complaining. Now we hear the Cook, the most unredeemed realist in the play, debunking greatness and praising the absence of virtues, while Anna Fierling makes up her mind about his offer. The song serves two functions, psychological and ideological. It gives the listening mother time to think and makes clear what goes through her mind; and it clarifies the leitmotif of the play to the audience. Virtues do not pay in this world, are dangerous, and "a man is better off without." We should not interpret this to mean that Brecht expounds here a philosophy of immorality and anarchy (as he sometimes came dangerously close to doing in his earlier days). The song simply reaffirms the credo of the Marxist: "in this world," i.e., at our present capitalistic stage of history, virtues are not possible, at least not in a consistent manner and to a high degree; but even in this world man cannot exist entirely without them. The wisdom of a Solomon, the courage of a Caesar, the honesty of a Socrates, the unselfishness of a Saint Martin are excessive and dangerous, the Cook tells us. Significantly, he does not mention mother love—a fact overlooked by all commentators on this scene. It seems to me that the love of a mother for her child, so frequently treated by Brecht, had for him something of the qualities of a given biological and social fact of life that is not acquired through an exertion of the conscious will, like a virtue. While Mother Courage listens to the Cook, she knows that she is neither wise, nor brave, nor honest, nor unselfish; but she is reminded that she is, and always has been, the mother of her children, of whom only Kattrin is still around. So she sticks with her. She has no choice.

The functional use of the songs, which were not always tightly integrated with the dramatic structure in the earlier plays, is only one indication of the mastery Brecht achieved with *Mutter Courage und ihre Kinder*. While his twelve scenes convey the overpowering impression of huge armies incessantly on the move in a never-ending war, the ever-present covered wagon effectively unites the few protagonists and gives added coherence to their specific actions. If it may be said that nothing characterizes the born playwright as much as his scenic imagination, that is, his ability to translate abstract ideas into concrete visual images, Brecht scores very high, indeed. Scene III, in which Mother Courage loses her honest son by haggling too long for his release and then is forced to view his corpse without showing signs of recognition, is full of an almost unbearable suspense and has an emotional impact of the most gripping kind. Scene XI, in which Kattrin climbs onto the roof of a farmhouse, beats her drum to warn the citizens of Halle, and is killed, has been called "possibly the most powerful scene, emotionally, in twentieth century drama" by a critic as knowledgeable and demanding as Eric Bentley.[5] Another sign of a dramatist's caliber—and to most theatergoers the most important one—is the ability to create memorable characters. Nobody who has seen *Mutter Courage* on a stage is likely to forget the tough, earthy, shrewd, and yet touching businesswoman and mother Anna Fierling; but Brecht

also succeeded in surrounding her with a number of sharply
sketched, three-dimensional minor characters: poor, pathetic,
children-loving Kattrin; the great womanizer and realist, the Cook;
the cynical and opportunistic Chaplain with a heart; the harlot
Yvette, who is the only one to get something out of the war and
ends up as a wealthy widow. There is one artistic achievement,
however, which only the compatriots of the German author can
fully appreciate: his extraordinarily rich and strong idiom. No
translation has managed to approximate the flavor of Brecht's
unique mixture of the most diverse prose components, through
which he tried to evoke the speech of the seventeenth century
but actually created a kind of artificial and highly original
language of his own. There are traces of Luther, Grimmelshausen, Hašek, Bavarian country fair barkers, Swabian dialect,
and the ungrammatical speech of South German peasants. Although John Willett correctly pointed out that "the very un-
smooth clarity at which Brecht aimed, . . . is not an uncommon
quality in our own language too,"[6] many puns and allusions in
the original German lose their pungency and wit in English translation. To give just one example: in Scene III, Mother Courage
reflects on the war in Poland, where she is at the time, and says:
"Die Polen hier in Polen hätten sich nicht einmischen sollen."
Since "einmischen" is a highly ironic expression for the reaction
of a people who are invaded, the Bentley translation, "the trouble here in Poland is that the Poles would keep meddling," falls
flat. When Courage continues: "anstatt dass die Polen den
Frieden aufrechterhalten haben, haben sie sich eingemischt in
ihre eigenen Angelegenheiten und den König angegriffen, wie
er grad in aller Ruh dahergezogen ist," Brecht obviously alludes
to Hitler's invasion of Poland in September, 1939, which had
occurred only a few weeks before he wrote these lines; but the
English version, "instead of keeping the peace the Poles attacked
the Swedish king when he was in the act of peacefully with-
drawing," both flattens and distorts the sentence. "To attack" is
not "einmischen," and "in aller Ruh daherziehen" is not "to with-
draw." It should be admitted, however, that Bentley, who did so
much for Brecht in America, translated him as well as can reasonably be expected from anybody who is not genuinely bilingual. Even without the original German text, sparkling with

hundreds of brilliant verbal facets, *Mutter Courage und ihre
Kinder* has conquered the stages of the world. The play has,
by now, become a recognized modern classic, and no less an
expert than Tennessee Williams is said to have called it the
greatest drama of our century.

II   Leben des Galilei
(Galileo)

No play illustrates more clearly the obstacles that stand in
the way of an interpreter who wishes to explain Brecht to American readers than his *Leben des Galilei*. First, there is the usual
problem of various versions, some of which are not available in
published form. Second, there is the annoying fact that the
English translation is not the one of which Brecht himself approved at the end of his life; it is considerably shorter than the
revised quasi-"official" German text on which most performances
throughout the world are now based. Third, the play has become
the favorite target of ideologically biased Brecht scholars and
critics whose intransigence has been compounded by the chaotic
state of published and unpublished versions and translations.
In addition to numerous articles and essays, *Leben des Galilei*
has even provoked one complete and one half book by the
Marxist scholars Ernst Schumacher and Werner Mittenzwei,[7]
and is the basis of Gerhard Szczesny's *The Case against Bertolt
Brecht*, an attempt to prove the playwright's "arrested ado-
lescence" by means of his presumably autobiographical stage
hero.[8] It is, therefore, necessary to summarize a few undisputed
facts before we deal with the play itself. Brecht was interested
in the figure of Galileo as early as 1933 but did not start writing
the play until 1938. After reading up on the historical scientist,
he wrote *Leben des Galilei* within a few weeks in November of
that year, having the accuracy of his astronomical and physical
descriptions checked by an assistant of Niels Bohr in Copenhagen and making a few changes in December after the German
physicist Otto Hahn had announced the splitting of the atom.
Since Brecht was already then thinking of moving to the United
States and aiming at an American production, he commissioned
Desmond Vesey to translate the play into English while he sent

the German original to Zurich, where it was not produced until 1943, however. Later, in Hollywood, Brecht befriended the actor Charles Laughton, who had liked *Schweyk* and who saw in Galileo a suitable part for himself. In December, 1944, both men embarked on a joint translation, which, after several interruptions, was completed one year later. The new version, ruthlessly cut upon Laughton's insistence, changes Galileo's character from a cunning hero who recants in order to safeguard his scientific discoveries into a coward who betrays the truth, and thus fails to set a moral standard for future scientists. As Brecht himself admitted, the dropping of the bomb on Hiroshima strongly affected his conception of Galileo's character.[9] The premiere of this English version took place in Beverly Hills on July 30, 1947, and met with little success. Without waiting for the New York performance in December, Brecht left for Europe. He later re-translated the English version and restored many of the passages cut in Hollywood, thus creating a final text which may be called an enriched and refined second version. This is the play as it is now generally known, printed, and performed throughout the world. During rehearsals with the Berlin Ensemble shortly before his death, Brecht made several additional cuts but no changes in the text. It is clear, then, that the Laughton version, by which most Americans know *Galileo*, can no longer serve as the basis for an objective evaluation of the play.

As we have already pointed out, *Leben des Galilei*, one of the recognized masterpieces of the mature Brecht, is written in the manner of the chronicle play. In fifteen scenes, we follow the physicist's career through a span of twenty-eight years, from 1609 until 1637. When we meet him first, he is already forty-six years old and an underpaid professor at the University of Padua, living with his daughter and a housekeeper, whose intelligent little son he likes to instruct. Frustrated because he must waste his precious time with excessive lecturing and private tutoring, he accepts the better conditions of a position at the court of the Medici in Florence. Galileo's findings tend to prove the theories of Copernicus, which run counter to the Ptolemaic system of the earth as the center of the universe. Although the Pope's own astronomer, Clavius, confirms Galileo's calculations, the Holy Office cannot tolerate an attitude which threatens to question the Church-proclaimed cosmic order and thus, conceivably, the religious, economic, political, and social order of the human world. A hedonist with a gigantic appetite not only for science but also for the good life, including food and drink, Galileo is told to lay off astronomy and to abstain from publishing. He restrains himself for eight years, but when a new Pope, known to be a mathematician and a liberal, ascends the throne, Galileo can no longer resist the intellectual temptations and resumes previously started research on sunspots. By doing so, he not only brutally drives away his daughter Virginia's conservative fiancé and breaks up her imminent wedding, but he makes the clash with the Church inevitable, all the more so since his subversive ideas begin to spread. The Pope no longer protects him and agrees to have him summoned to Rome by the Inquisition. In 1633 Galileo publicly recants when shown the instruments of torture. The remainder of his life he spends under house arrest in the country, forbidden to write and publish, guarded by the Inquisition, and watched over by Virginia, now a pious old maid. Gradually becoming blind, he is still consumed by compulsive craving for rich food and drink. When we see him last in Scene XIV, he is seventy-four years old and is being visited by his favorite pupil, who is on his way to Holland. Andrea, who learns that Galileo has secretly finished his main theoretical work, *The Discorsi*, and hidden a copy of it for him to smuggle abroad, is overwhelmed by admiration for his teacher, who, he now thinks, only recanted to complete his research. Galileo, however, rejects this view and accuses himself of having betrayed the truth and having failed to set an example for the world; he even refuses to shake hands with the younger man of science in whose ranks he no longer belongs. The final Scene XV (usually cut in most stage productions) shows Andrea carrying Galileo's book across the Italian border.

The best way to understand and appreciate *Leben des Galilei* may be to shed some light on Brecht's probable intentions. A dramatist rarely if ever merely aims at total accuracy when he chooses historical material; he must be judged by other criteria. Shakespeare's *Richard III* and Schiller's *Maria Stuart* are not superb dramas because they are important chapters in the history of England but because their creators effectively used historical characters and settings for their own, quite different purposes. Brecht is not the only one who saw certain similarities between the seventeenth and twentieth centuries; we have already observed the striking parallel between Mother Courage's war and Schweyk's wars. And who will deny that the contemporaries of a Kepler, Galileo, Bacon, Descartes, and Leibnitz were as conscious of living in a "new scientific age" as Brecht claimed we are today in the era of Marx, Freud, and Einstein? (He planned a play about Einstein, but did not get around to writing it.) In short, we may almost postulate that sooner or later Brecht *had* to write a play about the greatest physicist of the seventeenth century, and that his purpose would be to show the relevance of Galileo to our time. When Brecht worked on the script, he became increasingly aware of the dangerous alienation of ever more complex modern science from ordinary man. It is no surprise, therefore, to learn from Mittenzwei and Schumacher, who studied the unpublished materials in the Brecht Archives, that the playwright originally aimed at a positive folk hero who worked in close proximity to the people and who later deliberately recanted in order to get his ideas across. While I see no evidence that Brecht was motivated by Stalin's purge trials, as some critics have suggested, it seems highly likely that he was less interested in the recantation of his hero than in the fact that Galileo managed to complete his *Discorsi* under the eyes of the Inquisition. It seems to me that Brecht saw in Galileo's case a historical precedent for successfully spreading the truth despite secret police and the Gestapo. Marxist scholars are probably correct when they claim that *Leben des Galilei* was at first conceived as a political antifascist (i.e., anticapitalistic) play in historical disguise. It was Brecht's answer to an essay of 1934 in which he had prescribed five means for the dissemination of truth under terror: (1) the courage to write it, (2) the wisdom to recognize it, (3) the ability to use it as a weapon, (4) the proper choice of effective recipients, (5) the cunning to spread it.[10] Thus, the Galileo of the earliest drafts was a revolutionary scientist, deeply concerned with the life of the people and their miseries, and praiseworthy, above all, for his cunning. The title of the new play was to be taken from the famous legendary (but unfounded) saying "Und sie bewegt sich doch!" (And yet it, i.e., the earth, moves!); the notes refer to a "version for workers."

It speaks for Brecht's intellectual integrity and artistic maturity that in the completed first manuscript of 1938 his Galileo had already become a more complex character and also more in line with historical truth. He is still cunning and the great, admired hero because he has deceived the authorities by pretending to be blind while he secretly continued to write; and he craftily arranges for his manscript to be smuggled out of the country. But his recantation is no longer the result of a deliberate plan but due to his fear of death. Schumacher reports that, while an assistant of Niels Bohr, with whom Brecht discussed *The Discorsi*, approved of the recantation, "Brecht, however, was of the opinion that Galileo's recantation of his theory of the earth in 1633 represented a defeat, which was, in years to come, to lead to a serious schism between science and human society."[11] The significant admission of the Danish physicist, "I could never understand this point of view," may well have been an additional reason why even then Brecht's Galileo became less socially conscious and more of an "intellectual" than he was intended to be in the preliminary sketches. Galileo emerges as a contradictory and ambiguous man, in some respects resembling his modern creator; and it is for this reason that malevolent critics have drawn unflattering and often foolish inferences from his dilemma. Just as the splitting of the atom by Otto Hahn in 1938 sharpened but did not precede Brecht's notion of the moral responsibility of science, so the dropping of the bomb on Hiroshima (1945), while he worked on the English translation, was only the most visible and terrifying confirmation of that "serious schism between science and human society" which the playwright had already foreseen. He did not need to drastically change Galileo's character or the structure of his drama. All that was needed was to make the great physicist somewhat more negative by presenting the completion of *The Discorsi* more as the result of habit (he was as much a compulsive researcher as he was a compulsive eater) than a deliberate act of defiance, and finally to have him condemn himself unequivocally. Most changes, therefore, occur in Scene XIV when Galileo interrupts Andrea and (quoting Brecht's own comments) "proves to him that the recantation was a crime, and not to be balanced by the work, no matter how important." Brecht added: "Should it interest anyone, this too is the opinion of the playwright."[12] To paraphrase the change between the two versions, again in Brecht's own words: what was a "defeat" (the recantation), regrettable and to be condemned, has now become an unredeemable social "crime."

Leben des Galilei is as little a tragedy as *Mutter Courage*, unless we are willing to equate a scientist's thirst for knowledge and a businesswoman's greed with the tragic flaw or grain of evil of a Shakespearean hero. Brecht's Galileo is a sensuous man, and his ambiguity results from this trait. His voracious appetite is his strength and his weakness at the same time. He leaves a poorly paid but safe position in the Republic of Venice, which would have protected him from the Inquisition, for more money and more free time for research in Florence, although a friend has warned him of the greater influence of the Church there. That he is not a coward is shown in a scene, omitted in the Laughton version, in which he continues his work in the midst of a plague epidemic while everybody else flees. The Pope, who has no intention of destroying Galileo, only consents to having the instruments of torture shown to him because he knows that such a man could not stand the sight of them. In his great final speech, Galileo admits to Andrea: "I have come to believe that I was never in real danger; for some years I was as strong as the authorities, and I surrendered my knowledge to the powers that be, to use it, no, not use it, abuse it, as it suits their ends." In other words, in the last analysis Galileo recants because he misjudges the situation. When he later wrote *The Discorsi* under house arrest and defying specific orders, he simply did so because he could not help himself. His thirst for knowledge remained as insatiable as his appetite for the roasted goose we see him devouring at the end. No tragic hero he—and also, we must add, no Marxist one. Bentley put it succinctly when he wrote: "What Marxist historian would accept the notion that a Catholic scientist of the Seventeenth Century, whose best friends were priests, who placed both his daughters in a convent as young girls, was halfway a Marxist, resented convents and churchgoing, doubted the existence of God, and regarded his tenets in physics as socially revolutionary?" However, he added just as astutely: "But it is one of the open secrets of dramatic criticism that historical plays are unhistorical. They depend for their life on relevance to the playwright's own time—and, if he is lucky, all future times—not on their historicity."[13]

There is no question that, in the age of the hydrogen bomb, the morality of the scientist has become a theme of the greatest possible relevance, but the projection of a modern point of view and experience into a historical figure still constitutes a matter of legitimate criticism. Brecht himself was apparently never completely satisfied with *Leben des Galilei*, and still bothered by the recantation of his ambiguous hero when he worked over the script for a Berlin production shortly before his death. After completing the Danish version, he voiced misgivings about a certain opportunism that in his opinion had prevented "the planetary demonstration" the material demanded. His criticism then was entirely aesthetic and was directed neither against the plot nor against the characterization, but he felt that the play constituted a backward step in terms of the technical mastery of the new epic theater which he had achieved in the meantime. The fact that he compared his presumed "opportunism" with a similar one responsible for *Frau Carrars Gewehre* reminds us of our previous observation about the relatively straightforward realism of other anti-Nazi plays such as *Furcht und Elend des Dritten Reiches* and *Die Gesichte der Simone Machard;* it tends to confirm Schumacher's and Mittenzwei's notion of *Galilei* as a tool originally conceived for fighting Hitler. Brecht's criticism is no longer valid because the subsequent "official" version of the play is sufficiently epic to place it in the vicinity of *Die Mutter* and *Mutter Courage und ihre Kinder*. There are recited verses and projections before and, at times, at the end of scenes; there are many passages which seem to be directed to the audience as commentaries and are not needed for the dialogue onstage; there is a whole scene interrupting the action and only serving as an alienating device for enabling the audience to gauge Galileo's standing with the common people; and there is, finally, his unhistorical self-accusation, which establishes "the planetary connection" of the play's message. In short, the final *Leben des Galilei* qualifies as an anti-illusionary drama for "the children of the scientific age," in Brecht's own terms; the fact that he specifically used the play to illustrate certain points of his theory in *Kleines Organon für das Theater* (Short Organum for the Theater [1948]) proves this point. There still remains, however, the ambiguity surrounding Galileo's recantation, which in my opinion Brecht did not successfully resolve. Most readers and audiences will not agree with the playwright's stern verdict, and are likely to see only human weakness for which they can cite many mitigating circumstances. They sympathize with Galileo to the end, and disagree that they have witnessed how "a great hero" turned into "a great criminal" (Brecht's words). And this despite the fact that Brecht took great pains to emphasize Galileo's social concern and great popularity and his awareness of his own unique role in the history of science, which the full text (not the Laughton version) shows. It seems that Brecht overestimated the reasoning powers of audiences, who are supposed to see in Galileo the first physicist in history who was in a position to establish a credo for science such as Hippocrates had done for medicine, and whose betrayal must, therefore, be judged in the theological dimension of original sin. Niels Bohr's assistant who could not see Brecht's point before Hiroshima, unfortunately resembles most of his colleagues—and also government leaders—in the hydrogen era, who continue to carry on business as usual. The shrewd Hanns Eisler realistically summed up the current limitations for endowing historical figures with notions of contemporary relevance when he rejected the Galileo of the final version as superheroic and told his friend Brecht: "Let him eat at the end!"[14]

Why then is *Leben des Galilei* nevertheless generally considered one of the great plays of the modern theater, even by those who have reservations about its ideological validity? To begin with, it has an overpowering impact on any audience or reader: next to Mother Courage the Italian physicist is the most convincingly three-dimensional and complex stage character Brecht created, and he dominates most scenes with his intellectual charisma as strongly as his contemporary, the sutler woman, does on an earthier level. Galileo is inquisitive, intelligent, shrewd, and not above cheating, but also capable of generosity, a born teacher inspiring admiration and unstinting loyalty, naïve to the point of acting stupidly, egotistical, filled with a love of people and especially children, compassionate and yet brutal, a man of tremendous energy, obsessed with an almost maniacal curiosity, driven by an insatiable thirst for knowledge, and endowed with a Gargantuan appetite for everything, which, in the last analysis, accounts for his glory as well as his undoing. In short, he is an actor's dream, and one can easily understand why Laughton wanted to play him. He is surrounded by an entourage of minor characters whom Brecht etched out sharply and convincingly and with admirable economy. The highest praise, however, must be reserved for the characterization of Galileo's adversaries, the dignitaries of the Church, who are not shown as mean or stupid men but as intelligent, even sympathetic representatives of the authorities of the time; they are antagonists worthy of a great opponent. Despite the play's length, each scene serves a purpose in Brecht's design. When Laughton omitted Scene V, which shows Galileo's obsession with research prevailing over his fear of the plague, and when the New York production dispensed with the procession song in Scene X, which is indispensable for revealing the link between Galileo's discoveries and their theological and political implications, the artistic quality of Brecht's masterpiece was unjustifiably and severely damaged. In terms of visual splendor and inventiveness, Scene XII, during which the new Pope, the former cardinal and mathematician Barberini, with each new garment put on him gradually yields to the Inquisition's request for having Galileo shown the instruments of torture, is dazzling in its originality and stage symbolism. The subsequent Scene XIII, in which we wait, with Galileo's disciples, for the public announcement of his recantation (and hope with them that he won't recant) until the defeated and almost unrecognizable physicist makes his entrance, is full to the brim with dramatic and emotional tension; and then there is, of course, the crucial and climactic confrontation of teacher and pupil in Scene XIV. Most of all, however, there is the brilliance of Brecht's language, at once historically accurate (he used some of Galileo's own writings, famous for their clear and simple style) and elegant in a modern sense for its sophisticated and highly ironic flavor. Brecht almost, but not quite, overcame the obstacle of transforming the inherent dryness of mathematics and astronomy into an aesthetically pleasurable theater experience. Nobody has so far done better than he in putting a convincing and historically credible scientist on the stage, and this is no mean accomplishment per se. Growing demands for a new morality of the scientist in our time will lead to a still greater appreciation of Brecht's magnificent *Leben des Galilei*.

III   Der Gute Mensch von Sezuan
(The Good Woman of Setzuan)

In March, 1939, Brecht noted in his diary that he had resumed work on an old project of the late 1920's in Berlin, then called *Die Ware Liebe* (Love as Merchandise); and he added: "it gives me the chance to develop the epic technique and, finally to reach my standard again. No concessions are needed for the desk drawer."[15] The entry is revealing for several reasons: it confirms Brecht's dissatisfaction with the first version of *Leben des Galilei*, which he had just completed and considered "opportunistic," i.e., below standard; it also shows that the new play was not to be encumbered by considerations of immediate usability as a fighting tool or by the restrictions imposed by historicity. Brecht's desk drawers already bulged with unpublished manuscripts and untested plays, and although the fight against Hitler consumed his energies in those years to a large extent, he still managed to give highest priority to his development as a literary artist. He had come to see in the parable play the most suitable form for his epic theater; now was the time to apply to the new technique the mastery he felt he had gained in the meantime. When we consider the circumstances under which *Der Gute Mensch von Sezuan* (The Good Woman of Setzuan) was written, we must marvel at the playwright's concentration and dogged perseverance in the face of the most inopportune conditions. He started in Copenhagen while Hitler was dissolving Czechoslovakia in the spring of 1939, continued in Sweden while World War II was beginning, resumed work after his flight to Helsinki the next year, and finished the play in January, 1941, in his third temporary makeshift home in Finland. When Brecht came to America a few months later, no prospect for a production materialized, although Elisabeth Bergner and Anna May Wong were for a while interested in

playing the lead; it was again the faithful theater in Zurich
that staged the world premiere, in 1943. Bentley's first English
translation was published in 1948, and in that year the play saw
its first American performance at Hamline University in Saint
Paul, Minnesota. The first professional production was offered
by the Phoenix Theater in New York in 1956. Brecht himself
helped with the first West German staging in Frankfurt in 1952,
but did not live to see the Berlin Ensemble presentation five
years later. Today most Americans know the play through Bentley's revised adaptation, which he made for his own production
in New York; it is not a literal translation, being shorter than
the original script but faithful to its spirit. Brecht's epilogue,
in my opinion very important, is omitted but printed as an
alternative ending.

How to be good and yet to live: this is the problem that
Brecht's dramatic parable poses. If at least one really good
human being can be found, the world may be allowed to continue as it exists. Three gods, on an inspection tour to prove
this point—and thereby also to justify their own existence, I may
add—are given shelter for the night by the penniless prostitute
Shen Te, the only person in Setzuan who is willing to take them
in. The next morning the gods show their gratitude by giving
her some money, so that she may buy a small tobacco shop. Immediately, she is harrassed by all kinds of petitioners and para-
sites who threaten to bankrupt her. Unable to say no to anybody,
she invents a ruthless male cousin, Shui Ta, whose role she as-
sumes by means of different clothing and a mask. Shui Ta drives
the spongers away. As Shen Te she then meets an unemployed
pilot, Yang Sun, saves him from suicide, and falls in love with
him. When she learns as Shui Ta that Sun is only after her
money, with which he hopes to bribe his way into the position
of a mail pilot, she pretends that Shen Te is away on a journey
and resumes the role of a brutal businessman. Finding out that
she is pregnant, she is now all the more determined to make
sure that her future son may never go hungry. Shui Ta starts a
tobacco factory. Sun, whom she employs, soon rises to foreman
because he, too, is ambitious and ruthless. Shen Te's long absence arouses rumors and suspicion, especially on the part of
her friend, the water-seller Wang, who had first put the gods

in touch with her and who has remained in communication with them ever since. Shui Ta is arrested and brought to trial for the murder of Shen Te. The three gods reappear and act as judges. When they learn that Shen Te is still alive, they are overjoyed and satisfied that "the good woman of Setzuan" justifies the continuation of the world as it is. Shen Te confesses that she could only have survived by alternatively being the bad Shui Ta, and she adds:

> Find me guilty, then, illustrious ones,
> But know:
> All that I have done I did
> To help my neighbor
> To love my lover
> And to keep my little one from want.
> For your great, godly deeds, I was too poor, too small.

When she asks in despair how she can go on being a good person, the gods have only platitudes to offer. To her plea "I need my bad cousin!" their council is not a denial of the request but the ironically accommodating reply, "Once a month will be quite enough!" Shen Te's cry for help remains unanswered, and the impotent gods depart.

Brecht was very careful to place his parable in a setting which was sufficiently general and removed from the demands of historicity (*Leben des Galilei*) so that nothing would detract from the full impact of the message he wished to convey. His nondescript China, in which "there are still gods but already airplanes,"[16] stands for capitalistic society in its earlier phase everywhere. Man lives by exploitation, poverty and unemployment abound, and religion only serves to preserve the status quo. Whether we concede that Shen Te would hardly exist in a social-democratic but still capitalistic country like modern Sweden or whether we simply dismiss her as excessivly naïve, we cannot deny that the essence of capitalism is the competitive spirit, which only rewards ambition and aggressiveness. Whether we see in the three gods a representation of the bourgeois-Christian tradition or in their ineffectiveness a persiflage of German idealism, or whether we consider their impotence as a confirmation of Nietzsche's dictum that "God is dead," Brecht shows, at the end of his parable, that the departing gods are unable to solve Shen Te's problem "to be good and yet to live." They are quite satisfied with lip service to goodness and don't mind a little fraudulence now and then when they unashamedly consent to their good woman of Setzuan playing the part of the not so good Shui Ta from time to time.

Brecht does not offer a solution in his play, which is supposed to be a parable of life as most of us know it and in which a truly good person cannot survive; but the answer the audience is expected to give to the urgent questions posed in the epilogue is obvious: The world can and must be changed. As a Marxist, Brecht wished to take away the opium from the people, so that they could become strong and help themselves. The removal of religious blinders is the sine qua non for societal change, as Pelagea Vlassova and Joan Dark had already learned. Shen Te learns as little as Anna Fierling did, but the playwright hoped that the audiences would learn more. It might be interesting to recall in this connection that the children of Mother Courage were destroyed by their excessive virtues, while she herself went on living—just like Shen Te. Does that mean goodness is no virtue? Yes and no. I have ventured the notion that Brecht considered mother love to be a fact of natural life not requiring a conscious act of will; and I shall have to add now that, contrary to Freud and Christian dogma, he also believed simple goodness to be the natural state of man, which is only restricted and perverted by the mechanics of capitalist society. Shen Te finds it easy to act like a good person but difficult to change into Shui Ta; in one of his later poems describing a Japanese mask, Brecht says: "Sympathetically I observe / The swollen veins of the forehead, indicating / What a strain it is to be evil." The possibility suggests itself, therefore, that man should strive for a society of the future in which simple goodness (like simple mother love) will be possible. The excessive goodness of Shen Te will not be needed then and will be looked upon as a regrettable distortion of human behavior, provoked by capitalism, which is hostile to the natural inclinations of man. Galileo's verdict, "Unhappy is the land that needs a hero," can also be applied to Shen Te: Unhappy is the land that needs goodness as a virtue; that is, in excess. Seen in this light, Shui Ta symbolizes the paradoxical fact of our society: that to be good, man must also be bad. We are reminded of Mother Courage, who needed war in order to take care of her children. She becomes a bad person and loses the children, just as Shen Te becomes the cruel Shui Ta to act as "the angel of the slums" and to have a lover. She ends as "the tobacco king" and loses her man.

Whether we detect an ambiguity here or not, it seems clear to me that Shen Te is not a tragic figure in the accepted sense, as some critics have suggested. I disagree with Walter Sokel, for instance, who sees a special Brechtian tragedy expressed in the schizophrenia of his split characters and who states: "In order to realize his goodness man must renounce his goodness. His tragedy is that he can never effectively be what he naturally is."[17] I believe that Brecht would have rejected a view that makes, in essence, every member of the human race a tragic figure. We all know that we are not perfect and that we do not, nor ever will, live in a perfect world. To think otherwise makes man either insane or stupid, but not tragic. Shen Te is not the schizoid victim of unalterable God-given goodness, but a nice and not very bright girl who overindulges in natural kindness. In a better world, she would not need her brutal cousin Shui Ta but might come reasonably close to "effectively be[ing] what she naturally is." It is only capitalistic society that suggests to her the deliberate choice of an objectionable crutch for survival, which she, incidentally, freely chooses; and there is every indication that a changed Setzuan would have room for many good women. However, Brecht's case of a good person who cannot really be good in our present world is presented in such a universal and poetic manner that it is bound to touch almost any audience irrespective of the ideological platform of the individual spectator.

The plot of the drama consists of three sections chronologically presented and governed by Shen Te's three goals: to help her neighbors, to love her lover, and to protect her unborn child from want. Brecht reached the desired technical standard by superimposing the complexities of the epic technique in such a way that the whole action moves on three levels, or dimensions, as it were. First, there is the dramatic level, on which we follow Shen Te/Shui Ta's encounters and involvements with the people in Setzuan. Second, there is the philosophical level, consisting of the prologue and several interludes (after scenes I, III, VI, VII, IX) in which the water-seller Wang and the three gods reflect and comment on the events, usually in a more elevated "poetic" language and with the frequent use of songs. The third level is not visible in the text at all but is constituted by the reaction of the audience, which the playwright frequently solicits by means of direct appeals and questions, by making the spectator an invisible judge in the last trial scene, and by challenging him, in the epilogue, to find a solution, which the playwright deliberately withholds. Thus, the protagonists judge each other on level one; they, in turn, are judged on level two; and we, on level three, judge level one and, at the same time, level two judging level one. A multidimensional structure with shifts in perspectives, breaks in illusionary audience identification, suspension of time and action, has been created in order to make the parabolic presentation, which is simplistic almost by definition, appealing and challenging to the more intellectual audiences of the modern theater. All this, of course, would still mean very little if Brecht had merely developed the epic technique one step beyond *Leben des Galilei* without giving other evidence of his dramatic mastery. While it is probably fair to say that the characters of *Der Gute Mensch von Sezuan* are not as fully developed and interesting as Schweyk, Anna Fierling, or Galileo, Brecht again excelled in scenic invention and created many original and theatrically effective episodes. The special charm of the play, however, rests on a peculiar quality that is very rare in the theater and rather difficult to describe. I am referring to a stance of ceremonial politeness and distant human relations, expressed in an understated language of austere lyricism, which Westerners usually associate with Chinese culture and philosophy. It adds a new and rather unique tone to the rich orchestration of the Brechtian theater and seems eminently suitable to the form of the parable play.

IV   Herr Puntila und sein Knecht Matti
(Mr. Puntila and His Servant Matti)

Between his first and third stay in Helsinki, Brecht spent the late summer and fall of 1940 as a house guest on the farm of

Hella Wuolijoki, a well-known Finnish writer, who told him some stories about a rich landowner and translated a half-completed comedy, based on them, into German in order to gain his collaboration for the purpose of jointly entering a folk play contest. Brecht took up the challenge. Within a few weeks in September, he completely revised the material and wrote a play of his own which, though it did not win the expected prize in Miss Wuolijoki's Finnish translation, has since found a place in the repertories of many countries. Again we must marvel at Brecht's ability to block out the oppressive present while engaged in a literary project. This time he even surprised himself, as his workbook reveals: "It would be incredibly difficult to analyze a state of mind which causes me to follow the Battle of England on the radio and in the bad Finnish-Swedish newspapers—and then to write *Puntila*. . . . *Puntila* hardly concerns me, but the war totally; about *Puntila* I can write almost everything, but about the war nothing."[18]

It was not until the end of Brecht's American exile and after his return to Europe that the world premiere of *Herr Puntila und sein Knecht Matti* (Mr. Puntila and His Servant Matti) took place in Zurich (1948), with Brecht himself as co-director. His name was omitted from the program credits, however, because he did not have the work permit required by the Swiss police. One year later, after he had accepted the East German offer of his own theater, he chose the play for the opening production of the Berlin Ensemble. There have been many performances throughout Europe, but none in the United States as far as I know; and only two scenes of the English translation (Gerhard Nellhaus and Richard Grenier) have been published in a periodical. Despite the great popularity of the comedy, most critics and scholars have little to say about it and tend to see in it a pleasant but minor work of little weight. They overlook several factors, in my opinion. First, seeming "lightness" may be deceptive and only the appealing façade for a deeper meaning behind it; second, the truth revealed by laughter does not cease to be the truth because it is not revealed by tears; third, a mature dramatist who selects one of his plays for a very special occasion is not likely to choose a trifle. It is for these

reasons that I like to discuss *Herr Puntila und sein Knecht Matti*
among the masterpieces of Brecht's exile.

For social reasons, Puntila, a rich farmer, is about to marry
off his daughter Eva to a diplomatic attaché. A big drinker, he
is friendly, generous, and humane when under the influence of
alcohol, but selfish and mean when suffering from "attacks of
senseless soberness." While intoxicated, he hires several new
farmhands, gets engaged to four girls, treats his chauffeur Matti
as an equal and companion, and even wants him to marry his
daughter because he despises the priggish suitor. Sober, he
drives away the village women and the newly hired help he
does not need. Eva wants Matti, who attracts her, to compromise
her in the eyes of her fiancé, whom she finds wanting in manli-
ness. However, the diplomat's "debts are too great," and he
pretends not to have seen Matti emerge from the sauna cabin
after Eva. During the engagement party, Puntila becomes drunk
again, throws out the attaché, and offers his daughter to his
chauffeur instead. In a hilarious scene, Eva is called upon to
demonstrate her qualifications as the wife of a poor proletarian,
and, as is to be expected, she flunks the test. Sober again the next
morning, Puntila dismisses a "red" worker because his friends,
the lawyer and the clergyman, demand it; and he also resolves to
give up drinking. Determined to destroy his liquor supply and to
smash all bottles personally, he gets stone-drunk again in an
even more hilarious scene during which he raises Matti's salary
and promises him half of his wooded land. The next day, Matti
leaves in disgust because, as he tells the audience: "It's time
that your servants should turn their backs on you. They will
have found a good master only when they have become their
own masters." Since this day has not come yet, it is clear that
we must see in Brecht's play another Marxist presentation of
man's alienation from his true self in capitalist society.

Shen Te needed Shui Ta in order to be at least partly good.
Puntila needs a similar crutch to be at least partly human.
Whenever he is sober, he must conform to the role of the capitalist, from which he can only temporarily escape in the
state of intoxication. This means that, in the last analysis,
Puntila's sober state (his class-determined behavior) will always
prevail, and neither the audience nor Matti is fooled by his

drunken promises. The Marxist chauffeur knows very well that whenever his master allows himself an excessive share of intoxicated humanity it will be followed by an equally ugly relapse into his normal capitalistic state—witness the dismissal of the "red" worker right after the banquet—and Matti wisely leaves after the stoned Puntila has bequeathed half of his forest to him. As Ralph Ley has stated in a searching article, "the Marxist Brecht only affords to the spectator a minute glance of the world that is not yet, that world to come which must still be portrayed within the limits of the present reality."[19] Ley refers to the conversation between the minister's wife and the cook, whom the drunken Puntila forces to sit next to each other during the banquet, and who become engrossed in a discussion over the best way to preserve mushrooms. On the surface, it is only a very funny and innocuous little incident, but to a Marxist it is a "confrontation between persons of different classes who for the moment participate naturally but subconsciously in their common humanity."[20] For the same reason, Eva's marriage test, another of those class confrontations, must come to an abrupt end when her playful (more or less subconscious) participation in Matti's humanity is rudely interrupted. He slaps her on the bottom, and she is offended; i.e., in Marxist terms, "the minute glance of the world that is not yet" is over, and we all are reminded of "the limits of the present reality." Many more examples could be cited to show how carefully Brecht integrated humor and social significance in this play, which may be called the first genuinely Marxist comedy.

There is a subgenre in German drama which is called *Volksstück*, and has no exact equivalent in English. "Folk play" or "popular play" comes closest, but does not convey the historical reality the term has enjoyed in the German theater. One usually refers to a nonintellectual play with farcical, melodramatic, and sentimental overtones, written and staged by actor-playwrights for suburban audiences of the lower classes, flourishing in nineteenth-century Vienna, and occasionally still surviving in nonprofessional playhouses in Bavaria. It seems that Brecht's disagreement with the chief aesthetic theorist of the Stalin era, Georg Lukács, over the definition of "socialist realism" directed his attention to the almost forgotten and neglected genre. Several

published and unpublished essays of the late 1930's testify to the
controversy, and in 1940 he wrote "Notes on the Folk Play"
with specific references to the just completed *Herr Puntila und
sein Knecht Matti*. Since Brecht was frequently accused of being
a formalist, it is altogether possible that he wished to demonstrate his ability to write a truly "realistic" play by elevating the
deteriorated and crude *Volksstück* to a new, intellectually and
aesthetically satisfying, art form. The last time a serious and
acknowledged dramatist had succeeded in writing a modern
Volksstück was in 1925 when Carl Zuckmayer, Brecht's old
colleague, friend, and rival of the Berlin days, enchanted Germany with his coarse, bawdy, and hilarious comedy *The Merry
Vineyard*. Jost Hermand has convincingly argued that this work
is the secret model for *Herr Puntila und sein Knecht Matti*.[21]
The similarities in plot, characters, and incidents are indeed
striking. Moreover, we remember Brecht's penchant for writing
"antiplays" to already well-known dramatic works (*Baal, Eduard
der Zweite, Heilige Johanna, Frau Carrars Gewehre, Die Tage
der Commune*). The decisive difference between the two plays
is in their ending. While in Zuckmayer's romantic-bourgeois
fairy tale the daughter of the rich father gets her man of the
lower class, the proletarian Matti knows that the happy end of
a marriage would only be a momentary illusion, and he declines.
Brecht's characters escape the confining reality of their socioeconomic station as little as Chaplin's tramp in *City Lights*, who
is also subjected to the intoxicated humanity of his millionaire
friend, which does not last. It may be significant that Zuckmayer's once so popular play has disappeared from the theater
and Chaplin's film, which undoubtedly inspired Brecht, is as
fresh and timely as ever. The higher degree of social and psychological applicability, however, would still not justify our ranking
Herr Puntila und sein Knecht Matti among Brecht's masterpieces unless the artistic values of the comedy could also be
demonstrated.

This time we have no complex multilevel structure, but the
epic character of the play is achieved by the narrative technique
of presenting many, and often very broad and self-contained,
episodes. The playwright tells us several separate stories about
Puntila that are only very loosely tied to the main plot of Eva's

engagement. Some of the scenes can be drastically shortened
without harm to a performance, as Brecht himself suggested.
Only a minimal dramatic frame is provided by a brief prologue
and epilogue and the "Puntila Song," one stanza of which is
sung by the cook after each scene to which it refers. There is no
real beginning (Matti has already been in Puntila's employ for
five weeks), and we never learn whether Eva will marry the
attaché after the chauffeur has departed. The focus of Brecht's
attention on the stage is the confrontation of master and servant,
as the title correctly implies, and of the two it is Puntila who over-
shadows each scene. In his sensuality and delight in earthly
pleasure he is a kind of nonintellectual Galileo. He is also im-
aginative and shrewd, generous and mean, impulsive and cal-
culating, vacillating between moments of euphoria and depression. By comparison, Matti is less colorful, but he has a
Schweykian sense of humor, always remains cool and intelligent
even under trying conditions, and radiates a quiet dignity that
his master lacks. Martin Esslin's observation that "Puntila steals
the play"[22] is an overstatement; moreover, it would probably
leave Brecht cold, because in the capitalistic world he wanted
to depict it is of necessity only the master who can afford to be
colorful and not the servant. Even more than the fine characterization, it is the scenic inventiveness that makes *Herr Puntila
und sein Knecht Matti* a superior comedy. There is, for instance,
Scene V, where we simultaneously watch Eva and Matti in the
sauna cabin, presumably making love, and outside Puntila trying to divert the attention of the attaché, who, however, pretends not to notice what he thinks is going on. There is the long
banquet scene (IX) with Matti's extremely funny examination
of his master's daughter, who demonstrates her unfitness to be
a suitable wife of a proletarian. And there is, finally, the hilarious
Scene XI, during which Puntila, determined to be sober, becomes
stone-drunk, has Matti build a fictitious mountain (made out of
demolished expensive furniture), the peak of which (the table)
he then climbs in order to deliver a hymnical oration on the
beauty of the Finnish countryside. What distinguishes all of
these extraordinarily original and funny episodes from the
farcical level of only accidental or purely mechanical stage
business is their meticulously established social and psycho-

logical justification. Each incident grows out of the premises the playwright has built before, and each character acts according to the dictum "being determines consciousness," which even most bourgeois audiences accept, although Marx coined it. If, in that process, additional humor is extracted from a reversal of the traditional romantic happy end, all the better for a playwright who wants to put his notion across. This time it is the poor man who rejects the rich girl—and in how many comedies does this happen? Although still unknown in America, Brecht's play about a meaningful confrontation between a master and his servant in deceptively funny disguise has proved its appeal in the West. For the audiences in communist countries, where land reform has reduced the Puntilas to obsolete figures of purely historical interest, Brecht cleverly printed a timely reminder from the writings of Marx: "History is thorough and goes through many phases while burying her figures. The last phase of a historical figure is his comedy. . . . Why this turn of history? So that mankind may part from the past in serenity."

V   Der Kaukasische Kreidekreis
(The Caucasian Chalk Circle)

We have had occasion to observe that many Brechtian plays owe their origin to a curious combination of old and abandoned, or even forgotten, plans and sudden external circumstances prompting him to start, revise, or finish a work, which had occupied his mind before, in a relatively short time. We have also seen that neither adverse personal living conditions nor the gloomy prospect of a Europe conquered by Hitler could hamper Brecht's artistic pursuits. It is amazing, therefore, but hardly surprising that his most serene and cheerful play was written in Hollywood, a city he hated and in which he felt more uncomfortable than in any other of his many exile residences. The Austrian-born actress Luise Rainer was instrumental in getting Brecht a contract for adapting an old Chinese play for Broadway; having become famous for the lead in the filmed version of Pearl Buck's *The Good Earth*, she probably saw the chance for another fat part. Brecht, of course, strongly remembered the 1924 Berlin production of *The Chalk Circle*, an adaptation of a medieval Chinese play by his friend Klabund, in which one of his favorite actresses, Carola Neher, had scored a great success. He had already used the material when writing a story, *Der Augsburger Kreidekreis* (The Chalk Circle of Augsburg), in 1940. In addition, we should not forget that the older Brecht became increasingly fascinated with all things Chinese, including the philosophy of Confucius, Chinese history and fiction, Chinese acting (one of the sources for his V-effect), and the austere style of Chinese poetry. He sketched out the new project while on a trip to New York in March, 1944, and wrote, revised, and completed it within a few months. For reasons still to be discussed, he shifted the locale to Soviet Georgia and called the play *Der Kaukasische Kreidekreis* (The Caucasian Chalk Circle). The world premiere in Bentley's translation took place at Carleton College, Minnesota, in 1948; Brecht himself staged the first German performance with the Berlin Ensemble in 1954. There have been numerous productions since throughout the world, including successful ones in San Francisco and New York.

At the end of World War II, members of two collective farms meet to resolve a dispute about a tract of land, formerly belonging to a goat-breeding Kolkhoz and then abandoned to the advancing Germans. The neighboring fruit-growing Kolkhoz, whose members fought as partisans, submits an irrigation proposal for which the valley in question is essential. After some discussion, it is decided to give the land to those who will make it more productive: the fruit growers. Then they all enact the old legend of the chalk circle under the leadership of a famous singer, who hopes that "you will find the voice of the old poet also sounds well in the shadow of Soviet tractors." In feudal Georgia, some centuries ago, the Grand Duke was overthrown and one of his Governors killed; his wife fled and abandoned her little son. Grusha, a kitchen maid, saved the baby and took it to her brother's place in the mountains. Although she was engaged to the soldier Simon, she allowed her brother to arrange a marriage of convenience to a presumably dying peasant in order to give the child a name and a home. After two years a counterrevolt brings the Grand Duke back. The Governor's widow also returns and claims her estate, which she can, however, only obtain as the mother of the legal heir. Soldiers find

Grusha and the infant and seize them before she can explain the situation to Simon, who has come back from the war. The ensuing trial is conducted by Azdak, a drunken village scribe and rogue, who had been appointed judge by the rebellious soldiers two years earlier and who has been newly confirmed by the Grand Duke, whose life he once saved. Azdak has a circle of chalk drawn on the ground and the infant placed in the middle of it. When the two contesting women are asked to pull him toward themselves with all their strength, Grusha immediately releases her hand; she cannot bear to hurt the child. Azdak awards the child to "the right mother" and also divorces Grusha, so that Simon may marry her. The play concludes with the following lines spoken by the singer, who thus reestablishes the connection between past events and the present:

> Take note what men of old concluded:
> That what there is shall go to those who are good for it,
> Children to the motherly, that they prosper,
> Carts to good drivers, that they be driven well,
> The valley to the waterers, that it yield fruit.

Der Kaukasische Kreidekreis is divided into six parts, or broad sections, most of which consist of several episodes linked by the comments of the singer onstage. Its structure is highly complex and more epic than that of any other Brechtian play. There are three plots, or tracks, running partly simultaneously and partly chronologically, ingeniously interwoven and all merging at the end. Plot I involves the members of the two postwar collective farms arguing, commenting, playacting, and also reacting as audience on the stage in Part I, as well as the singer with his helpers and musicians, who visibly accompanies all six parts. Plot II comprises Grusha's story, spanning two years and mainly played out in Parts II, III, and IV up to the child's capture. It ends with the suspense-creating question of the singer: "Who will decide the case? / To whom will the child be assigned? / Who will the judge be? A good judge? a bad?," whereupon Plot III provides the answer by shifting to Azdak and showing, in Part V, his judicial qualification and experience during the same span of two years during which we have followed Grusha's tribulations. The concluding Part VI of the trial, containing the experiment with the chalk circle, thus chronologically and structurally unites all three plots and, at the same time, provides the intellectual and emotional climax of the whole play. The epic character of the work is enhanced by the visible presence of the singer, whose storytelling function far exceeds the use Brecht made of commentators or choruses in other works. The singer narrates a novel in three parts, as it were: Book I, Grusha; Book II, Azdak; Book III, the Trial. No longer the omniscient "I" or majestic "we" of bourgeois fiction in the nineteenth century that have been eroded by the modern novelist's self-doubt and skepticism, Brecht's singer acts, nevertheless, as the omnipotent manipulator of modern epic devices. He introduces and initiates action, transforms past events into contemporary happenings, interjects himself and then withdraws, poses questions and anticipates answers, expands, compresses, and juggles time and space, and reveals to the audience the complexity of human beings who often act differently from the way they talk or even think. Thus, Brecht, who wished to change man through his theater, as Marx told the philosophers they should, reinforced his notion of the changeability of the world by means of a stage narrator who is omniscient on the basis of scientific social Marxism and omnipotent in terms of the modern epic devices at his disposal. The result is a kind of "dramatic novel," a term with which Brecht's mentor Feuchtwanger had already experimented in the early twenties, i.e., prior to the fully developed concept of an epic theater. *Der Kaukasische Kreidekreis* is a narrative rendering of the world, conceived in the spirit of the born storyteller or genuine raconteur, who, as the singer in the play, creates, organizes, and controls the chapters of his tale unfolding on the stage in a mode and with a technique that are truly epic.

We have seen that for the Marxist Brecht a so-called virtue is determined by its social value; the better the society, the fewer the virtues required, so that in utopia Shen Te will exist without Shui Ta and Puntila will be human without the bottle. It stands to reason that even a Brecht who had mellowed with the times would not adapt an old legend about motherhood and superimpose on it a questionable fairy-tale judge without a deeper purpose. This is where the opening scene of the collective farms comes in. It is somewhat apart in style and language from the rest of the play, and I confess that I once argued in an article[23] that this was an essentially non-Marxist play to which Brecht later added a prelude for political reasons. I was strengthened in my wrong assumption because Bentley's first English translation did not contain the prelude, which is also omitted in many productions, especially in the West. In the meantime, however, I have learned that Brecht first wrote the prologue in 1944 (and also an epilogue which he later eliminated), and that Bentley left it out, upon Brecht's request, for tactical reasons related to his appearance before the Un-American Activities Committee in 1947.[24] Irony has it that it is precisely the prologue, with its "unrealistic" and stylized presentation of an exotic Soviet Russia, that embarrassed East German and Russian critics. We can dismiss this criticism as primitive socialist realism, but we must take issue with the British scholar Ronald Gray, who points out, somewhat sarcastically, that Azdak's decision for Grusha is hardly analogous to the awarding of land to fruit-growers and that the communist message "is only loosely connected with the main plot."[25] It seems unfair to equate the "bad" mother with the goat-breeding Kolkhoz; but is this really Brecht's point? In the Marxist view of family relations, it is the child's welfare that counts, and the good mother is the socially useful mother. A claim purely based on biology is as rejectionable as inherited private property. It is relatively insignificant whether or not goat-breeders who once owned the land are decent folks and the Governor's wife is an unsympathetic bitch; the only question before the judge is the proper upbringing of the child in societal terms. Azdak, a true Marxist, is fully aware of the issue at stake. Shortly before he orders the test with the chalk circle (which is only the outward manifestation of a true mother's rightful behavior) he tells Grusha: "I don't believe he's your child, but if he *were* yours, woman, wouldn't you want him to be rich?" Whereupon Grusha remains silent, but the singer (in a beautiful demonstration of the V-effect at its best) tells us what goes on in Grusha's mind and what we already know from Shen Te: in capitalistic society, it is wealth that corrupts and makes man bad:

> Had he golden shoes to wear
> He'd be cruel as a bear

Evil would his life disgrace.
He'd laugh in my face.

Carrying a heart of flint
Is too troublesome a stint.
Being powerful and bad
Is hard on a lad.

Then let hunger be his foe!
Hungry men and women, no.
Let him fear the darksome night
But not daylight!

At the beginning of the trial, Grusha had already told the judge why the child should be assigned to her and had summed up her claim with the only relevant argument in social terms: "I brought the child up to be friendly with everyone, and from the beginning taught him to work. As well as he could, that is. He's still very little." In other words, Brecht's play, despite its deceptively mellow tone, is still meant to be a Marxist parable; he needed the frame of the prologue and (after he eliminated the epilogue) the concluding words of the singer in order to show that we are not witnessing a charming old tale with no relevance to us. Without the prologue, Azdak's judgeship remains a bizarre incident and, at best, a meaningless exception. From the vantage point of an already functioning socialist society that is not utopian (Soviet Russia in the prologue), it becomes "a brief golden age, almost an age of justice." The accent is on "almost," because Azdak must operate during the capitalistic pre-stage of wars, upheavals, injustice, greed, and bribes and is, of necessity, tinted by all of this just as Schweyk and Puntila, and, to use Ralph Ley's words again, he can only provide "a minute glance of the world that is not yet, that world to come which must still be portrayed within the limits of present reality."[26] The prologue reminds the audience that there is a future reality that is already in the process of being reached. This explains in my opinion the dry and matter-of-fact language of the collective farmers and their friendly, polite, rational way of dealing with their controversies. After the prologue had been cut in the West German production at Frankfurt, Brecht incorporated the initial scene with the new title "The Dispute about the Valley" into his play as the integrated Part I. There is no doubt that the Kolkhoz scene is ideologically and structurally needed, but one may still question whether Brecht fully succeeded in fusing his political intention and the dramatic execution. While I disagree with Bentley, who dismisses the prologue as a bouquet for Stalin and calls it "a non-Russian Stalinist's view of Stalin's Russia,"[27] I concur with his judgment that Part I (the prologue), against Brecht's intentions, does not stay in the mind of audiences because it lacks sufficient weight. When John Fuegi, conversely, tries to show the play's tight structure by describing the beauty of Brecht's Berlin production, including his casting of the singer and Azdak with the same actor,[28] he only proves, in my opinion, that the shrewd director Brecht was at times able to improve on the playwright Brecht.

Audiences are less likely to ponder the particular Marxist ethos of *Der Kaukasische Kreidekreis* than to appreciate the many delights of one of the most charming and poetic plays of the modern theater. There is the strong, calm, brave, shrewd, commonsensical, compassionate, decent, naïve, angry, and cheerful Grusha, who will move even the most blasé spectator. And then there is the super-Schweyk Azdak, the corrupt, scandalous judge, full of folksy wisdom, coward and hero, a rogue, a cheat, and yet a man with a heart. He is one of the most delightful characters Brecht ever created, and nobody will ever forget him. For those who look for deeper meaning and possibly even for religious symbolism in their dramatic heroes, there is the strong implication that Azdak is also meant to be a satirical Christ figure in a rotten world of greed and violence, while Grusha with the child she did not bear alludes, of course, to the Virgin Mary. Many scholars have pointed out pertinent biblical passages and scenic situations, too numerous to be accidental.[29] In purely theatrical terms, there is a wealth of original and effective episodes, such as Grusha crossing a severely damaged bridge in flight from the Ironshirts; the hilarious wedding scene on a divided stage with the presumably dying bridegroom lying in bed in one room and his mother, Grusha, the priest, and the guests haggling, celebrating, and gossiping in the other; Azdak proving his fitness to be a judge; Azdak adjudicating a case of rape and the case of a doctor who treated a patient without fee; and the final trial scene with the test of the chalk circle. In addition, there are countless and often elaborate pantomimes betraying a very keen theatrical sense, rare in the overly intellectual climate of modern drama: Grusha's first encounter with the little boy, when she watches him hesitatingly before picking him up, probably inspired by a similar pantomime in Chaplin's *The Kid*, is just one example; or one may point at the many incidents silently enacted while the singer in a corner of the stage comments on them. The language (except in the prologue) has a lyrical quality culminating in many songs throughout the Grusha plot, while the Azdak action is appropriately counterbalanced by a starkly realistic, vulgar, Schweykian prose idiom. The greatest attraction of the play is its unique charm, which is achieved by a blend of contrasting linguistic levels and variegated stylistic devices so that the spectator is enchanted without ever losing himself in mere escapism. He roots for the poor servant girl and is spiritually uplifted by the thought that sterling characters like her are possible in our terrible world. He laughs at a judge who is unlike any other judge he has ever seen in a robe; and yet he can hardly fail to notice that the man's often hilarious decisions are based on a deeply pessimistic philosophy resulting from the failure of a revolution that did not create a new world but only new masters. Throughout the play, we view the events with a laughing and a weeping eye, as it were. We know that the older Brecht came to appreciate and to include more and more the category of "the naïve" in his evolving theory of the epic theater.[30] He achieved this new naïveté with the writing of *Der Kaukasische Kreidekreis*, the most charming and cheerful of his last great plays through which he redeemed the hard years of his long exile.

CHAPTER 6

The Modern Theater Is the Epic Theater

WHAT John Willett stated a decade ago is still true of the average theater lover who is not a Brecht specialist: "In Western Europe and the United States it [Brecht's theory] is better known than either his plays or his actual methods of production, and for this reason it is often wrongly assumed that these merely follow the lines which it—or its interpreters—lay down."[1] Ignorance and erroneous notions abound, partly caused by half-understood slogans such as "alienation effect" and "non-Aristotelian theater," and compounded by a proliferation of new publications which include both Brecht's own often repetitious and overlapping theoretical writings and an ever-increasing number of studies by critics and scholars. It is, therefore, not my intention to enter the competition by unduly stressing the theorist of a presumably new Brechtian drama. I only wish to dispose of the most frequent misconceptions and to summarize what appear to be Brecht's major theoretical concepts inasmuch as they aid a better understanding of his artistic intentions and achievements. After all, Brecht's claim to fame—and possibly to immortality—does not lie in the fact that he happened to write more *about* his craft than most literary artists, but in the fact that he had the creative endowment of a gifted playwright, stage director, and poet.

Anybody studying philosophy is aware of the German penchant for systematizing. Kant's famous three critiques and Hegel's published lectures are outstanding examples of this tendency; but even minor German scholars frequently force their notions into the rigid schema of a systematic arrangement. This also applies to literary historians, and may explain why German scholarship frequently appears ponderous and pedantic to foreigners. Brecht knew this and even made fun of heavy-

footed professorial musings at times, but he nevertheless per-
petuated the German tradition by theorizing about his own
intentions too much, too lengthily, and too repetitively. He paid
for his love of Hegel, as it were, and, to a smaller degree, for
that of Marx. At the end of his life, he fully realized the misunderstanding and confusion his excessively polemic and doctrinaire writings about the theater had caused in the minds of
people who often read them without recourse to his plays. When
during rehearsals an actor in 1953 asked him, "How is it that
one comes across so many accounts of your theater (most of them
hostile ones) which give no idea at all of what it is really like?,"
he disarmingly replied: "My own fault." His subsequent explanation may serve as the best starting point for illuminating
some of the most frequent misconceptions of the so-called
Brechtian epic theater:

These accounts, and much of the hostility too, apply not to the
theater that I practise but to the theater that my critics read into my
theoretical essays. I cannot resist sharing my technique and ideas
with the reader or spectator; and that has to be paid for.

So far as theory goes, I offend against the inflexible rule that the
proof of the pudding is in the eating—which happens to be one of my
own favorite principles. . . . My whole theory is much naïver than
people think, or than my way of putting it allows them to suppose. . . .
I wanted to take the principle that it was not just a matter of interpreting the world but of changing it, and apply that to the theater.
The changes, great or small, that ensued from this intention (which
I myself only slowly came to admit) were all changes within the
framework of the theater, so that, of course, a whole mass of old
rules remained wholly unaltered. It was in that little phrase "of
course" that my fault lay. I hardly ever got around to mentioning
these still valid rules, and many who read my hints and explanations
imagined that I worked to abolish them. If the critics could only look
at my theater as the audience does, without starting out by stressing
my theories, then they might well simply see the theater—a theater, I
hope, imbued with imagination, humor, and meaning—and only when
they begin to analyze its effects would they be struck by certain in-
novations, which they could then find explained in my theoretical
writings. I think the root of the trouble was that my plays have to be
properly performed if they are to be effective, so that for the sake of
(oh dear me!) a non-aristotelian dramaturgy I had to outline (calamity!)
an epic theater.[2]

In essence, these remarks reveal a Brecht who adapted Schiller's classical German concept of the theater "as a moral institution" to the modern world. Whereas Goethe and Schiller believed in the ennobling and humanizing function for the individual of art which would have to take precedence over, and become the prerequisite for, societal changes, the disciple of Marx wished to usurp the role of the philosopher, who, instead of merely interpreting the world, would place the theater at the disposal of his attempt to change it. Art in general and drama in particular were to aid in the process "of making the world more habitable." Since Marx, with his economic-political orientation, is the chief informant of Brecht, his theater is bound to result in a "political institution," just as Kant's metaphysical idealism sustained Schiller's belief in a moral in-stitution. Because Brecht was not a systematic thinker, some of his contradictions and exaggerations must be charged to the special conditions and occasions which provoked them. One cannot even say that Marx primarily inspired Brecht's theories; he only confirmed and fortified some of the notions the play-wright had held before. The sociologist Fritz Sternberg, under whom Brecht began his study of Marxism, put it succinctly when he said in 1927: "It was not through Marx that you came to recognize the decline of the drama. It was not through Marx that you came to speak of the epic theater. For, let us put it quite gently, Epic Theater, that is you, dear Herr Brecht."[3]

It follows that Brecht's theoretical writings must be taken with a grain of salt and seen as that which they were meant to be in most cases: retroactive and not always reliable com-ments on his presumed intentions, records of past rehearsals and performances, and instructions for potential directors of future productions. They cannot, and should not, be separated from Brecht's plays; and most misconceptions are due to the unsophisti-cated and patently false notion of the systematic creator of a grandiose theatrical theory who *also* happens to have written a few plays (and some of them in violation of his own rules). It is also no longer feasible to make a clear break between the youthful anarchist and the mature playwright who presumably formulated his theory under the influence of Marx. Perceptive critics such as Bentley have long ago pointed out that from the very beginning there is a clearly traceable unity in Brecht's thinking and writing; the previously quoted remark by Sternberg only confirms it. Neither would it be correct to agree with those who argue that the older Brecht was in the process of abandoning his theory altogether, and that only death prevented him from doing so. Finally, there are the published reminiscences of an old friend of Brecht, Rudolf Frank, who claims to have advised the young author of *Eduard der Zweite*: "You know that they will chalk up against your plays the fact that you have broken the rules, until you have succeeded in bracing them with a new theory of your own. Invent a theory, dear Brecht! When Germans get a theory, they swallow everything else."[4] While I cannot get as incensed as Frederic Ewen about the insinuation of a Brecht inventing his theory as a kind of fraud for boosting his plays, I find it unlikely that a playful remark made in 1924 should have triggered a lifelong habit of theorizing. It seems quite plausible to me that the shrewd young playwright might have been intrigued by his friend's admonition—it may have appealed to his sense of fun and penchant for mystification—but I find it sounder to assume that, on the whole, Brecht's epic theater constitutes his serious attempt to devise a theoretical basis for rescuing the art form of drama in our time.

I A Short Brecht Glossary

Alienation: *Entfremdung* in German, used in the Marxist sense by Brecht: man is alienated from his true self in bourgeois industrial society because he does not control the means of production.

Catharsis: The main effect of tragedy, according to Aristotle; by identifying with the dramatic protagonist, the spectator is purged while experiencing the emotions of fear and pity.

Culinary: Brecht's characterization of the traditional bourgeois theater which, at its best, has the same temporary effect as a lavish meal in a luxurious restaurant.

Dialecticize: A verb suggested by Brecht shortly before his death to describe his playwriting and directing efforts. To dialecticize means to focus on the contradictions inherent in events and characters in order to make them more lively.

Empathy: The projection of the spectator's personality into the character of the dramatic protagonist. The original German word, *Einfühlung*, suggests affection, passion—i.e., emotional involvement rather than rational conclusion.

Epic Theater: The term, used by Brecht for the first time in 1926, did not originate with him, although it is generally applied to his work today. It was already in the air when Brecht moved to Berlin in 1924 and was first used in connection with revolutionary experiments by Erwin Piscator. However, many playwrights and composers produced new plays and musical compositions in those years which have since been labeled epic (Stravinsky, Pirandello, Claudel), and others have followed in their footsteps (Wilder, Miller, Becket).

Formalism: A designation for undesirable and experimental efforts in any of the arts deviating from the narrow canon of socialist realism. Brecht's own work was frequently considered formalistic and this is the reason why he was little performed in Russia during his lifetime. In the thirties, Brecht engaged in a debate on realism with the most celebrated communist aesthetician, Georg Lukács, who, significantly, only approved of Brecht's minor nonepic plays: *Frau Carrars Gewehre*, and *Furcht und Elend des Dritten Reiches*. It is a safe guess that Brecht's work would have been dismissed as formalistic had not his international fame presented the authorities with the embarrassing need for tolerating him.

Functional Art: In the twenties, many artists, poets, and composers tried to make art a functional part of life. The terms *Gebrauchslyrik* and *Gebrauchsmusik* (for the poetry of Erich Kästner and the music of Hindemith) testify to this tendency of making art useful, which culminated in the famous Bauhaus Movement. Brecht contributed to these efforts with the didactic plays of his middle period.

Gestus: The Latin noun is difficult to translate into English. Willett defines it as "at once gesture and gist, attitude and point: one aspect of the relation between two people, studied singly, cut to essentials and physically or verbally expressed."[5] Since, as we have seen, actions determine character or, in

Brecht's words, "all feelings must be externalized," each person and each scene has its own basic social gestus, a kind of physical leitmotif or shorthand in terms of deportment, facial expression, rhythm, mannerisms, speech patterns, etc. The style of directing and acting, therefore, as well as the language of the playwright, must be gestic. The term also explains the importance of music for Brecht's theater, as music is particularly suited to bringing out the gestic goals of the epic theater. Thus, Kurt Weill confirms Brecht's theory as follows: "Music has one faculty which is of decisive importance for the presentation of man in the theater: it can reproduce the gestus which illustrates the action on stage, it can even create a kind of basic gestus which forces the actor into a definite attitude which precludes every doubt and every misunderstanding concerning the relevant action."[6]

Historize: Since Brecht rejects the concept of a basic human character that makes man act and react in a predictable way in keeping with unchanging timeless qualities, he aims at showing the specific circumstances responsible for a man's actions in a given situation. As Brecht states: "Historical incidents are unique, transitory incidents associated with particular periods. The conduct of the persons involved in them is not fixed and 'universally human'; it includes elements that have been or may be overtaken by the course of history, and is subject to criticism from the immediately following period's point of view."[7] The consequence for a modern theater is that playwright and actor must concentrate on the responses of stage characters relative to specific situations and periods—that is, they must historize.

Mimesis: Imitation or representation, especially of human speech and behavior, by the actor (Greek: *mimos*) in tragedy, according to Aristotle. Since it makes possible, and aims at, the spectator's empathy by creating illusion, it is one of the basic concepts of the Aristotelian theater which Brecht rejects.

Misuk: Motivated by a distaste for Beethoven's symphonies, which reminded him of "battle paintings," Brecht invented the term "misuk" for the music he liked and desired for his plays. According to Hanns Eisler, misuk is not decadent, or formalistic, but popular to the highest possible degree; it does not shut out the mind and does not lead to a pell-mell of jumbled emotions. The best example is probably Weill's "misuk" for *Die Dreigroschenoper*.

Naïve: Toward the end of his life, Brecht praised the concept of the naïve as the most concrete aesthetic category. Naïve in his sense stands for: full-blooded, contradictory, lively, more to be felt than rationally understood. In a conversation with one of his assistants, Brecht regretfully reveals that he had not mentioned the naïve in his theoretical writings because he had taken it for granted.[8] The remark shows (1) that it was provoked by the doctrinaire and inflexible cultural climate of Ulbricht's East Germany, and (2) that Brecht's theater was more traditional than it is usually conceded to be.

Scientific Age: Modern man is a child of the Scientific Age, which has made him, above everything else, inquisitive, skeptical, and critical. His pleasures, including his theatrical experience, must correspond to these character traits.

V Effect: The key concept in the Brechtian theater. It means the activity playwright and actor must engage in to achieve the desired effect of historization. An incident or action will only appear to me as unique, i.e., as a one-time event in history, if and when I observe it from a distance and cease to take it for granted. I must be brought to the point of finding it strange. V stands for the German *Verfremdung* and means "to make strange." Although the term is often translated as "alienation," one usually thinks of the latter in the sense of "alienating from" (modern man is alienated from his work), and I consider "estrangement," "making strange for a person," the better translation. Brecht used it for the first time around 1936 after he had come across the Russian equivalent (the word *ostrannenie*) in the writings of the formalistic critic Victor Shklovsky. Thus he found one of his most important concepts confirmed and defined by a known aesthetician, just as Marx had once provided the theoretical underpinning for vaguely felt social notions in his younger years. Reinhold Grimm and others have convincingly argued that the V effect is the one structural device that gives unity to Brecht's writing and directing.

II *Brecht's Major Writings on the Theater*

As early as 1918, Brecht published drama reviews in local newspapers of his native Augsburg, and at the time of his death in 1956 he was still engaged in refining and revising his views on the theater. The sum total of his essays, notes, conversations, dialogues, poems, model books, and fragments touching on various aspects of dramatic theory and stagecraft already fills many volumes, and no end is in sight, since there is still unpublished material in the Brecht Archives in Berlin. A brief description of some of the most pertinent theoretical writings may help the general reader who is not a specialist to understand Brecht's concern, to follow the development of his thinking, and to judge the validity of his epic theater as a general model for drama in the modern age.

Most critics consider Brecht's notes to the opera *Aufstieg und Fall der Stadt Mahagonny,* published in 1930, to be the earliest and most complete comment on his intentions. Their importance certainly would seem to be emphasized by the provocative title *Das moderne Theater ist das epische Theater* (The Modern Theater is the Epic Theater). Although the piece is seemingly concerned with opera, the central part of it contains a chart in which Brecht illustrates a shift of emphasis which he believed was taking place between traditional theater and some post–World War I efforts by himself and a few other pioneering young playwrights. Since Brecht equated the former with dramatic theater per se and the latter with epic theater (the theater of the future), the article has since become the most quoted testimony for the Brechtian theater and probably the only one with which those who do not read German are familiar. The chart reads as follows:

Dramatic Form of the Theater	*Epic Form of the Theater*
the stage embodies an event	narrates it
draws the spectator into an action	makes him an observer, but ...

consumes his capacity for action	awakens his capacity for action
allows him to have emotions	demands decisions from him
provides him with experience	provides him with knowledge
the spectator is drawn into a plot	the spectator is placed opposite it
suggestion is used	arguments are used
feelings are preserved	are propelled into perceptions
man is assumed to be known	man is the object of the inquiry
man unalterable	man alterable and altering
suspense about the outcome	suspense about the progress
one scene exists for another	each scene for itself
linear development	in curves
natura non facit saltus (nature does not leap)	*facit saltus* (leaps)
the world, as it *is*	the world, as it *becomes*
what man ought to do	what man is forced to do
his instincts	his motivations
thinking determines being	social being determines thinking

Most readers have ignored Brecht's footnote, "This table does
not show absolute antitheses but mere shifts of accent,"[9] but
since he overstated his distaste for the traditional theater of
illusion, which all too often drugs an audience's intellectual
capacity with overemotional empathy, his own theater has in-
correctly been equated with unfeeling rationalism ever since.
It should also be pointed out that the younger Brecht must be
seen in the special context of the German cultural scene in the
1920's, which determined his influences and colored his dislikes.
The old-fashioned declamatory style of provincial actors had
already enraged the young reviewer in Augsburg, for instance,
and so had the relatively lavish subsidy of often mediocre opera
productions throughout Germany. It explains his own attempts
at a new kind of contemporary opera, his collaboration with
modern composers like Hindemith and Weill, and the fact that

his most famous early pronouncement on his own theater appeared in appended notes to an opera. We should also add the strong antibourgeois feelings that Brecht shared with most intellectuals and artists of his generation; they received a new impetus when most bourgeois critics in Berlin severely panned the innovative and provocative productions by the leftist directors Erwin Piscator and Leopold Jessner, whom Brecht admired. Traditional theater, both state-subsidized and commercial, more and more became to him a public manifestation of despised bourgeois virtues, such as sentimentality, gushing emotionalism, and the mindless upholding of the status quo.

There were other influences which an alert young writer in the Berlin of the twenties could hardly escape. We have already mentioned most of them in the first chapter: dislike of the "O Man" exclamation by the older, expressionistic dramatists, Americanism to be felt for the first time, a new interest in sport (boxing, bicycle racing), the techniques of the silent movies, the emergence of a more detached and cool "Neo-Factualism" among certain German writers, Behaviorism, and the novel as an exciting new form for expansion and experimentation (Joyce, Döblin). In addition, I would like to mention another strong impetus for the theorizing young playwright from the provinces who was both fascinated and repelled by the big city in which he found himself: I am referring to his awareness of urbanization and its attendant consequences for modern civilization, which Brecht scholars have not sufficiently explored, in my opinion. Not only did the young Brecht locate many of his plays in big cities (Berlin, Chicago, London) and chose the revealing title *Lesebuch für Städtebewohner* (A Reader for City Dwellers) (1930) for his second collection of poems, but there are also numerous remarks in his notebooks indicating that he considered urban consciousness and life-style one of the crucial new phenomena of our time. Around 1926 he characterized his own writing efforts with the following words: "My heroic landscape is the city, my point of view relativity, my situation the moving of mankind into the big cities at the beginning of the third millennium. . . ."[10] What he called "relativity" when he had admittedly not yet read Marx is undoubtedly just a cipher for a cool, detached, skeptical point of view, which he was then in the process of acquiring, and which he came to equate with the posture of the scientist. Urbanization, as Brecht saw it, is one of the undeniable new features of the modern world; science is the other and even more important one, because it is gradually usurping man's whole mode of thinking, acting, and reacting. The task of the playwright is, therefore, to bring the theater, which in Brecht's opinion has remained stagnant since 1830, up to par with modern consciousness. When he designed his chart in 1930 (and even more so when he revised it in 1938), science to him had chiefly become sociology or, more specifically, the study of Marx and the discovery of dialectics. Only the more exacting standards of the narrative technique, developed with the aid of modern technology (film, revolving stage), could do justice to the more rational demands of the modern mind. By changing worn-out habits of theatergoers and creating new audiences, the dramatist felt that he could aid the philosopher (Marx) in changing the world.

In 1938, the same year in which Brecht revised the above chart, he wrote a short piece which very simply and most concretely illustrates how his new theater was supposed to differ from the traditional one. In the essay *Die Strassenszene* (The Street Scene), with the significant subtitle *Grundmodell einer Szene des epischen Theaters* (A Basic Model for an Epic Theater), he chose as his starting point a traffic accident at a street corner and compared an eyewitness who explains what happened to the type of new actor he desired. Brecht stated: "The bystanders may not have observed what happened, or they may simply not agree with him, may 'see things a different way'; the point is that the demonstrator acts the behavior of driver or victim or both in such a way that the bystanders are able to form an opinion about the accident."[11] If we go one step further and assume that the eyewitness is called to testify at a subsequent trial before a jury, we have the basic situation of the Brechtian theater; and it is, of course, no coincidence that real, implied, or imagined trial scenes abound in many of his plays. The writer's task is to assemble his material as objectively as possible and without preconceived notions of the likely outcome, so that the audience can rationally respond like a jury and make up its mind without taking sides. To make this possible, the actor (witness) must restrict himself to the task of demonstration and never lose himself entirely. This does not mean that he should be without emotions, but it requires a new kind of representation, the V effect, in which a certain distance is always maintained and careful weight is given to what is more and what is less important. It follows that the creation of illusion is no longer the aim of the new theater, whose audience remains aware that it is witnessing a conscious act of repetition. The model of the street scene also shows that character is entirely derived from actions. This is a break "with the orthodox theater's habit of basing the actions on the characters and having them exempted from criticism by presenting them as an unavoidable consequence deriving, by natural law, from the characters who perform them."[12] The example of the street scene further points to another prerequisite of Brecht's epic theater: its practical relevance in social terms. Thus, the function of the theater has been significantly changed. It is now didactic, and while Brecht was aware of the need to link his social concern with the requirements of an aesthetics of drama, he was not yet able to solve this task in 1938. Although he directly asked, "What about the epic theater's value as art?," he evaded a logically convincing answer by changing the question to "Can we make use of artistic abilities for the purposes of our street scene?," to which it is virtually impossible, of course, to reply with a "no." It was not until a decade later that the fifty-year-old Brecht attempted a reconciliation of Marx and Aristotle.

Kleines Organon für das Theater (A Short Organum for the Theater [1948]), written in Zurich before Brecht's return to Germany, is generally considered his most important theoretical work. The title and the composition of the relatively brief piece (one long essay in seventy-seven short paragraphs) are suggestive of his already-mentioned habit of claiming famous ancestors and writing "antipieces." Aristotle comes to mind, with whose *Poetics* Brecht had taken issue ever since he called his own dramatic efforts "non-Aristotelian." In addition, we may safely assume that Francis Bacon's *Novum Organum* inspired the title. Not only had the English contemporary of Galileo originated the saying that "knowledge is power" and was, as the

founder of the modern inductive method, a celebrated enemy
of Aristotle, but he had specifically defined and enumerated bad
thinking habits as "Idols of the Theater." The connection between life—thinking—theater—idols—Aristotle was not lost on
Brecht. The likely influence of the eighteenth-century French
philosopher, playwright, and art critic Denis Diderot should
also be mentioned; during the thirties Brecht had even tried to
found a Diderot Society. He was also mindful of the fact that
no German dramatist since Lessing had challenged the Aristotelian premises of Western drama. Moreover, the label "epic"
theater, in contradistinction to the categories of Aristotle's "dramatic" theater, seemed to call for a new definition and discussion
geared to abandoned concepts and his newly emerging position.

While Brecht, in his *Organon*, still aims at changing the
world, i.e., at teaching the audience a social lesson, his didacticism is now subordinated to aesthetics; and the theater has
become a form of art. Its main function is now said to be
entertainment, the giving of pleasure. "From the first it has been
the theater's business to entertain people, as it also has of all
the other arts."[13] It so happens that modern consciousness is
permeated by science more than by anything else: ergo, theatrical entertainment, too, must respond to this new challenge.
In its human representations, the stage must satisfy the greater
demands for factual truth and the increased awareness of new
complexities, or it ceases to be pleasurable. Only the epic form,
not restricted by the Aristotelian unities of time and place, can
provide the needed precision techniques. The catharsis of tragedy,
the purging from pity and fear which gave pleasure to the
ancients, is replaced, as it were, by the pleasurable sensations
of a modern skeptic who learns something new, especially in the
realm of social relations, "where darkness still reigns" because
the new scientific approach (i.e., Marxism) has not been applied
to society yet. Brecht links science and art through the aim he
assigns to both: to make men's life easier, "the one setting out
to maintain, the other to entertain us." The current theater,
however, is not equipped to do the job; a new style of presentation, which will correspond to the critical faculties of contemporary audiences, has to be created, and the major part of Brecht's
essay deals with the consequences of this shift for playwrights,

directors, and actors. It is interesting to note that Brecht was
forced to agree with Aristotle by retaining the story (action,
plot) as the heart of the theatrical performance, for, as he
states, "it is what happens *between* people that provides them
with all the material that they can discuss, criticize, alter."
Therefore, he no longer used the term "'non-Aristotelian drama"
in discussing his own efforts, which were now seen in the
context of a "theater of the Scientific Age."

III *Is the Modern Theater Really the Epic Theater?*

The evaluation of Brecht's theory of the theater greatly de-
pends on the interpretation of the phrase "Scientific Age," and
it is here that I disagree with those Brecht scholars who equate
the term with "the Age of Marx." They argue that the playwright
was exclusively thinking of the sociological consequences of new
scientific attitudes that had started to emerge in the nineteenth
century, of which Marx's *Das Kapital* was seen to be the first
significant work applying standards of pure science to human
society. His book has become a classic, in the sense that communists often refer to the writings of Marx, Engels, Lenin, and
Mao as "the works of our classics." In other words, these critics
consider Brecht's Marxism to be his overriding concern and
main inspiration for both his plays and his dramatic theory.
While I do not dispute Brecht's firm Marxist orientation in a
general way, I believe that his kind of Marxism must be viewed
in the light of several additional factors. I have already alluded
to his teacher Sternberg's observation that Brecht was not a
systematic thinker; and there is considerable evidence that he
was frequently prone to one-sided, excessive, and stubborn
statements and arguments. It is also generally conceded today
that he was mainly attracted by, and drawn to, the short philosophical writings of the younger humanist Marx rather than to
the older, economist author of *Das Kapital*, which Brecht may
or may not have studied systematically and thoroughly. Expressed
differently, it was Marx the disciple of Hegel, who had taught
him the dialectical method, whom Brecht appreciated most. I
don't deny that Brecht put the resulting dialectical materialism
at the service of teaching his audience a critical awareness of

the changeability of the social order, that is, of preparing it
for the change of the world according to Marx; but it seems
to me that he continued to reserve his highest appreciation for
Hegel, with whom the concept of dialectical thinking had
originated. There is no doubt in my mind that the humorous
flavor of much of Brecht's writing, for instance, is a direct result
of Hegel's dialectics (there is no humor in Marx). In his still
untranslated *Flüchtlingsgespräche* (Conversations among Refugees), the following statements about Hegel are to be found:
"He had such a sense of humor that he could not conceive of
something like order without disorder.... His book on Logic is
one of the greatest humorous works of world literature.... I
never found a person without a sense of humor who did understand Hegel's Dialectics."[14] This reminds us, of course, of the
following sentence in *Puntila*: "A person without humor is really
no human being at all." In other words, Brecht's antitragic view
of life, based on the ultimate perfectibility of the social world,
seems to have been influenced less by Marx's specific teaching
of class struggle than by Hegel's broader concept of dialectic
thinking. This explains—as Brecht's assistant Manfred Wekwerth
confirms in an article—that the old Brecht, had he lived longer,
would have replaced the term "epic theater" with the term
"dialectic theater" altogether.[15]

There is additional evidence that Brecht did not only have
Marxism in mind when he coined the term "Scientific Age." As
early as 1928, he wrote in a newspaper "about the tremendous
difficulty of raising the theater to the level of science";[16] and
the context makes it clear that he was not just speaking of
sociology then. In a radio discussion, Brecht once characterized
the naturalistic drama as follows: "It developed from the bourgeois novel of Zola and Dostoevski, which, in turn, signified the
invasion of science into the realm of the arts."[17] A few years
later, while discussing the mental state of a murderer, he stated
in an essay: "Modern psychology, from psychoanalysis to behaviorism, acquaints me with facts that lead me to judge the
case quite differently, especially if I bear in mind the findings of
sociology and do not overlook economics and history. You will
say: but that's getting complicated. I have to answer that it *is*
complicated."[18] If we add to this Brecht's interest in (and rela-

tively thorough knowledge of) astronomy and physics in preparation for *Galileo*, his plan of a projected Einstein drama, and
the impressive list of scholarly books he read in exile, we must
conclude that he did not conceive of the Scientific Age as a
mere cipher for Marxism but really used the term in both its
literal and general sense. When he described the introduction
of the footnote to the theater as one of his aims, or remarked
that modern audiences ought to get the same experience as
readers who can turn back the pages of a difficult book, he
was simply paraphrasing habits that modern science has created.
Who is seriously prepared to argue with Brecht's observation
that nothing has affected, and is still affecting, our times more
than science with all its consequences in terms of new knowledge, modes of thinking and behavior, and general life-style?
I was, therefore, not surprised when during an interview in 1966
even Helene Weigel and Elisabeth Hauptmann, devoted communists themselves, confirmed my notion that, in their opinion,
Brecht did not equate Marxism with science, which remained
to him the broader and overriding concept signifying the most
powerful modern experience.

If we thus conclude that the term "epic theater" essentially
describes efforts of playwrighting and staging which are in
tune with science-oriented modern consciousness, we must, indeed, come to the conclusion that "the modern theater is the
epic theater." Brecht, then, appears to be in the mainstream
of most literary tendencies in the twentieth century: the emergence of the novel as the most powerful and popular literary
genre, the gradual disappearance of "the well-made play," the
introduction of narrative techniques to the theater by leading
dramatists from Pirandello and Claudel to Wilder, Beckett,
Dürrenmatt, Frisch, Miller, and Weiss. Common to all of them
is an awareness of greater complexities, which can only be
accommodated by the less restricted devices of the storyteller.
Traditional plot sequence is replaced by free manipulation of
time and space, resulting in the use of flashbacks; the simul-
taneity of events is brought out in various ways; the frequent
shift of perspectives tends to underline the relative character
of an individual action; and the storyteller becomes the visible
commentator on the stage, who sometimes even takes part in

the action itself. We have already seen that Brecht considered the retelling of a street accident by an eyewitness as a proper, and even basic, model for his kind of theatrical presentation. We may accept this as additional evidence of his epic inclinations, especially when we remind ourselves that these purely narrative tendencies found their scenic realization in many of his plays in the reenacting of a story before a court or tribunal. While it is thus true that the modern theater has become an epic theater of which Brecht was one of the most influential pioneers, Mordecai Gorelik's limiting comment is also true: "To date, at least, there have been no examples of completely Epic plays, whether by Brecht or anyone else. Some plays are more Epic than others, depending on how much they tell of the wider social background of their personae. . . . Brecht considered his own plays to be the first steps in the direction of a specifically Epic drama."[19] And yet, one senses a difference between Brecht's brand of epic theater and that of the leading Western playwrights I named and whom he liked. It is in their views regarding the function of the theater in which they seem to differ.

Brecht wanted the theater to do what Marx suggested the philosophers ought to do: not just to interpret the world but to change it. He always remained a schoolmaster, a rationalist in the tradition alive from Aristotle and Horace to the men of the Enlightenment, who held the view that learning is useful and that the useful is aesthetically appealing. Entertainingly presented instruction is pleasurable. Since the skeptical and critical stance of the modern scientist has replaced the catharsis of the ancients, the theater must aim at satisfying the new sense of inquisitiveness in order to remain a viable institution. In contrast to the pure scientist who is mainly concerned with the nature of things, the theater is concerned with the actions of men. It must show them in as scientifically valid a way as possible, and this, in turn, means in the light of Marx, who was the first and most influential thinker to apply scientific methods to the social world. So far so good, provided the playwright avoids too narrow a presentation of the socioeconomic premises which inform him. In this respect, Brecht succeeded well, with only very few exceptions; his plays are not more Marxist than Shakespeare's dramas can be said to be feudal or

Molière's comedies absolutist. The fact that he was, and still is, more widely produced in capitalistic countries than in the communist orbit testifies to Brecht's artistic greatness. The additional fact that his theory has found practically no following in the communist world does not necessarily speak against it but simply illustrates the continuing predominance of officially ordained socialist realism, which in theatrical terms means the method of Stanislavsky. It only illuminates one of the major ironies underlying the Brechtian theater: that it is more appreciated by well-educated middle- or upper-class audiences than by members of the proletariat, for whom it was mainly intended. The bourgeois fellow traveler Brecht who fought illusion on the stage labored himself under a lifelong illusion concerning the audience of workers he wished to reach. However, even if we assume, for the sake of argument, that Brecht had succeeded in appealing to and moving the average little man, the question still remains of whether or not artistic experience—an aesthetically pleasurable performance in the theater—will lead to social or political action. Brecht's assumption that it does is unsupported; moreover, his own notion of the function of art has been ambiguous.

Despite Brecht's dislike of opera, he still defended its existence as an irreplaceable drug for the society of 1930 in his "Notes to *Mahagonny*," and he borrowed his supporting arguments from Freud's *Das Unbehagen in der Kultur* (Civilization and Its Discontent) of the same year: "The life imposed on us is too hard; it brings us too many agonies, disappointments, impossible tasks. In order to stand it, we have to have some kind of palliative."[20] In other words, art appears as something to make life bearable, not unlike religion, which Marx viewed as opium for the people. In the same footnote quoted by Brecht, Freud speaks of the pseudo-satisfactions offered by art, and he comes very close to Marx when he continues: "Such drugs are sometimes responsible for the wastage of great stores of energy which might have been applied to bettering the human lot." Interestingly, this is precisely the same essay in which Freud rejects communism on psychological grounds because, as he sees it, aggression is part of basic human nature and will not disappear with economic satisfaction. Even after Brecht had become an ardent Marxist, he seems to have been plagued by some doubts concerning the

essential goodness and perfectibility of man, as I have had
occasion to point out repeatedly.[21] If so, then the simplistic
teaching function of the theater had also to be adjusted to a
more sophisticated theory of dramatic art in which the fun
derived from sports in the 1920's was elevated to a full aesthetic
experience resulting from viewing a play. As early as 1940, when
concluding his theoretical dialogues *Der Messingkauf*, Brecht
came to acknowledge the priority of aesthetics over politics when
he wrote about his own theories: "There is no question of the
theater thereby losing its old functions of entertainment and
instruction; they actually get a new lease on life."[22] By that he
meant that the Aristotelian catharsis, which had been the prerequisite for aesthetic pleasure at a time when the theater was
still part of a ritual, now had to be replaced by the entertainment derived from satisfying modern man's awareness of his
domination by science. In Brecht's own words: "Concern with
reality sets the imagination off on the right pleasurable road.
Gaiety and seriousness revive in criticism, which is of a creative
kind. Altogether it is a matter of taking the old religious institution and secularizing it."

It seems that a few years later, when Brecht worked on the
Organon (which he considered his final theoretical work), he
became aware of the ambiguity remaining in his position. He
reread one of Schiller's essays and noted with amusement that
his great predecessor had also started from the premise that
the business of the theater is to give pleasure, but that for
Schiller, pleasure without morality was inconceivable. Brecht
added: "Therefore morality does not have to be pleasurable in
order to be admitted to the theater, but pleasure must be moral
in order to be admitted to the theater. I myself am doing something quite similar with the concept of learning when I simply
equate it with one of the pleasures of our time."[23] Brecht apparently came to realize that he had changed Schiller's assumption of moral pleasure into a similar claim of questionable
validity when he endowed the act of learning with the qualities
of an aesthetically pleasing experience. A more realistic assessment should have told him that what was true for him was not
necessarily true for modern man in general. We may add that
the subsequent assumption of the Brechtian theater is even

more questionable: the leap from pleasurably gained new knowledge to an actively sought change of society. The evidence so far has contradicted Brecht. The audiences most in need of societal changes have either not attended performances of his plays at all or have remained least affected by them, while his most appreciative capitalistic, and largely bourgeois, spectators have demonstrated little willingness to change the world upon leaving the theater. The truth is that Brecht's definition of the playwright's task has been as little accepted as Marx's admonition to the philosophers. Brecht apparently noticed this fact with some annoyance toward the end of his life, when he told Ernst Schumacher in 1955: "I must admit that I did not succeed in making clear that the word 'epic' of my theater connotes a social category and not an aesthetic-formal one. I am presently engaged in making some addenda to the *Organon* and I seriously ask myself whether it would not be best to drop the term epic theater altogether."[24] Since Brecht was too intelligent not to have known that, contrary to his statement, his efforts in the *Organon* had been specifically directed toward placing his theater firmly in the realm of aesthetics, the above remark shows his continuing difficulty in trying to reconcile Marx with Aristotle. If, despite the unresolved and basically unresolvable ambiguities of Brecht's theory, the epic theater has come close to being the modern theater, this is due, in my opinion, to his overriding notion of the "Scientific Age," which enabled Brecht to subordinate his Marxist credo to a broader concept held by most contemporaries irrespective of their socioeconomic and political views.

CHAPTER 7

The Poet beneath the Skin

ON the last day of a Brecht symposium held at Rutgers University in 1971, John Willett opened a lecture with the following sentence: "At the end of it all we come back to the poet, because you cannot really appreciate the playwright Brecht, or even perhaps the theatrical director, let alone the theoretician, without realizing that he was a poet first, last, and all the time."[1] Willett was then speaking as the editor of a forthcoming first full English selection of Brecht's poems which, however, is not yet available in this country. Only a fraction of Brecht's poetry is currently accessible to American readers: a total of eighty-six poems in two separate bilingual editions, not counting a few additional songs in the published versions of those plays that have been translated. By contrast, Brecht's *Collected Works* in German contain more than twelve hundred different poems on almost eleven hundred pages, not counting the rejected earlier versions and hundreds of verses discarded by their creator before publication. These startling figures are indicative of the sad fact that an Anglo-Saxon reader who does not know German is in no position to appreciate and evaluate the poet Brecht adequately. And yet, many scholars and critics consider his to be the most powerful German lyrical voice since (or even including) Rilke. Leading poets of our time, such as Auden, Spender, and Pasternak, felt drawn to translate him; Willett comes to the conclusion that it is precisely Brecht's poetic genius that also gives his plays whatever distinction they may have. He only reiterates what the influential German editor Willy Haas had already expressed in the twenties and what Hannah Arendt repeated in the sixties. The playwright, was, above all and foremost, a poet at heart, or, to borrow Willett's felicitous title of the above-mentioned lecture: "A Poet beneath the Skin."

Although Brecht published many poems in magazines and newspapers scattered all over Europe, he only prepared three selections in book form, and it is remarkable how much material he withheld altogether during his lifetime. Since it was the wild young man who burst upon the literary scene with a vengeance, so to speak, the mature and older Brecht is still considerably less known and recognized as a poetic voice, both in Germany and abroad; and the reasons for this neglect are mainly political. In trying to do justice to the achievement of a poet who not only was amazingly prolific at every stage of his career but also went through recognizable phases of literary development and growing maturity, I shall treat Brecht's poetry under three headings, which, in rough chronological order, indicate the main phases of his topical concerns and stylistic endeavors. If in my presentation, the first one tends to overshadow the others, the almost total absence of the older Brecht's poetry in translation is the obvious reason. Since I do not feel apt to render Brecht's poems into adequate English myself, I must depend on the available work done by Bentley and Hays, which, while highly laudable, falls considerably short of approximating the stark uniqueness of Brecht's original language.[2]

I *In the Shadow of Baal*

Willy Haas, editor of *Die literarische Welt*, Germany's most prestigious literary journal in the twenties, after discussing the beginnings of Brecht's dramatic career, adds the following significant sentence: "Let us take a deep breath now, because in 1927 there appeared a little book which established Brecht's lasting fame as a very great poet: a small and yet great book, the book of poems and songs with the title *Die Hauspostille*." A little later he adds the rhapsodic statement: "In this small volume there are cantos and verses which are as great, as mysteriously great as anything ever sung by man."[3] Haas only expresses a sentiment shared by many German scholars and critics as well as by Eric Bentley, who says in the preface to his own bilingual edition of *Die Hauspostille* (Manual of Piety): "Arguably, it is one of the best of all books of modern poems and certainly it is Brecht's best book of poems."[4] The original

German title is indicative of two tendencies, both characteristic of the early Brecht and the period in which the book first appeared. Historically, a *Hauspostille* is a book of prayers and other devotional literature for use in the home; the title was obviously chosen to mock religion and shock the bourgeois. Furthermore, it suggests the subordination of personal poetry to a communal purpose, i.e., a functional use, similar to the operatic efforts of Hindemith and Weill and the goals of the Bauhaus Movement in the twenties. Accordingly, the book is divided into sections such as "Supplications," "Spiritual Exercises," "Chronicles." It is here where the wild and anarchistic young Brecht, who projected himself into the fictitious Baal on the stage, fully released his lyrical voice. Not only does the book contain the "Chorale of the Man Baal" from the play, but we now know that Brecht and his youthful gang literally lived some of its scenes in and around Augsburg and that all poems in the book precede—and many accompany—the first and second drafts of the play. The shadow of Baal clearly lingered over Brecht's first selection of poetry.

Thematically, one may distinguish among three different types of poems in *Die Hauspostille*, with the ballads and legends forming the first group. The influence of Kipling and Villon is most noticeable, and to a lesser degree that of Wedekind. The heroes are the damned and rejected, the outcasts of society, viewed with affection, compassion, and also envy. Sometimes the tone is factual, even deliberately dry and impersonal like a newspaper account, as in "Von der Kindesmörderin Marie Farrar" (Concerning the Infanticide, Marie Farrar), which opens as follows:

> Marie Farrar, geboren im April
> Unmündig, merkmallos, rachitisch, Waise
> Bislang angeblich unbescholten, will
> Ein Kind ermordet haben in der Weise:
> Sie sagt, sie habe schon im zweiten Monat
> Bei einer Frau in einem Kellerhaus
> Versucht, es abzutreiben mit zwei Spritzen
> Angeblich schmerzhaft, doch ging's nicht heraus.
> > Doch ihr, ich bitte euch, wollt nicht in Zorn verfallen
> > Denn alle Kreatur braucht Hilf von allen.

(Marie Farrar, born in April,
No marks, a minor, rachitic, both parents dead,
Allegedly, up to now without police record,
Committed infanticide, it is said,
As follows: in her second month, she says,
With the aid of a barmaid she did her best
to get rid of the child with two douches,
Allegedly painful but without success.
    But you, I beg you, check your wrath and scorn
    For man needs help from every creature born.)
                       [Translated by H. R. Hays]

The affinity to Neo-Factualism is, of course, unmistakable here, just as it was in the third version of *Baal* in 1926. At times, the style of journalistic reportage may become mocking, as in the poem about another murderer, the boy Jacob Apfelböck, who killed his parents without apparent motive:

    Im milden Lichte Jacob Apfelböck
    Erschlug den Vater und die Mutter sein
    Und schloss sie beide in den Wäscheschrank
    Und blieb im Hause übrig, er allein.

    (In the mild daylight Jacob Apfelböck
    Struck his father and his mother down
    And shut them both into the laundry chest
    And he stayed in the house, he was alone.)
                    [Translated by H. R. Hays]

The subtitle "Oder die Lilie auf dem Felde" (Or the Lily of the Field) with its biblical allusion makes clear that a deliberate parody was intended.[5] Most often, however, the legends, ballads, or chronicles in Brecht's first book of poetry are hymnical and ecstatic evocations of the spirit of adventure, glorifying the strength and cruelty of nature and the exuberance of living at the edge of the abyss. There is the adventurer, "sick from the sun, and gnawed at by the rainstorms," who is forever seeking "the country where there is a better life"; and there is the sailor,

    Ohne Hut und nackt und mit eigenen Haien.
    Er kennt seine Welt. Er hat sie gesehn.

Er hat eine Lust in sich: zu versaufen
Und er hat eine Lust: nicht unterzugehen.

(Naked and with his sharks and without a hat.
He knows his world. He has looked into that.
And he has one desire left: to drown.
And he has one desire: not to go down.)
[Translated by E. Bentley]

The world which is revealed by the poet in his first book of
verse is neither kind nor nice nor comfortable, but brutal,
often dangerous, and always precarious; it is largely an outdoor
world for tough men: soldiers, sailors, pirates, and adventurers.
These men are what they are because they live close to nature,
which to them *is* the world. Consequently, we find in the *Hauspostille*, next to the ballads, many poems with nature mirroring
and symbolizing the transitoriness of all life, doomed to end in
rot and decay sooner or later. If there are any idyllic times, they
are significantly experienced while "you must just lie in ponds
or rivers like water-plants in which pike make their home"; i.e.,
by swimming through waters polluted by algae, mud, and sea-
weed, or by nakedly climbing in trees

Slowly and blackly in the evening air.
And in the foliage await the nightfall
With wraith and bat hovering about your brows.

Inspired by Rimbaud,[6] the poet finds relief by imagining himself
to be a ship, of which he sings:

Swimming through clear waters of many seas
Beneath red moons, beside the sharks, I freed
Myself from gravity and destination.

Idyllic moments, however, are rare and brief in a world in which
every living creature is ultimately doomed to be devoured by
nature. After Cortez's men died exhausted by their futile battle
with the jungle, "the forest ate the meadows up in a matter of
weeks." A man desperately holding on to a tree in his defiance
of death "Died like a beast with its claws in the roots," and of
the ship, mentioned above, fishermen said, before it went down:

Something was moving, bright with seagull dung,
Full of algae, water, moon, dead objects,
Silent and broad toward the washed-out sky.
[Translated by E. Bentley]

Nowhere did the young Brecht voice his lament about the eternal decay of life and nature's propensity for changing everything into carrion in more perfect lyrical terms than in the poem "Vom ertrunkenen Mädchen" (On the Drowned Girl), the last stanza of which reads:

Als ihr bleicher Leib im Wasser verfaulet war,
Geschah es (sehr langsam), dass Gott sie allmählich vergass
Erst ihr Gesicht, dann die Hände and ganz zuletzt ihr Haar.
Dann ward sie Aas in Flüssen mit vielem Aas.

(When her pale corpse rotted in the water
Very slowly God forgot her bit by bit:
First her face; her hands then; then last of all her hair.
In carrion-carrying rivers she was carrion.)
[Translated by E. Bentley]

It is not only the drowned girl that God forgot; again and again these poems express the young Brecht's bitter notion of the bad memory of Heaven. With sadness, at times with bitterness, and most often with defiance and cynicism, the poet sings of a world forgotten and forsaken by God. I am, therefore, inclined to consider religion the third theme of *Die Hauspostille;* even though it comes across only implicitly at times. It seems inconceivable to me that a writer who is in the habit of evoking the name of God, who reveals an intimate familiarity with the Bible, who models individual poems after hymns, prayers, and psalms, should be labeled nonreligious or indifferent to religion. Even violent renunciation would seem to indicate a concern that the true agnostic lacks. When Brecht parodied a well-known Protestant church hymn and carefully (i.e., ironically) started each stanza with "praise ye" while in reality meaning "woe," he cried out in a spirit which can only be called religious, as, for instance, the third stanza reveals:

> Praise ye the tree that from carrion shoots
> whooping toward Heaven!
> Praise ye the tree!
> Carrion that feeds it, praise ye!
> But never cease to praise Heaven.
> [Translated by E. Bentley]

Sometimes, the religious implication is veiled, as in a poem about a "man in violet" who sucks blood like a tick. Only after pondering the last stanza will the casual reader conclude that the man in violet is, of course, no other but a priest, of whom it is said:

> An keinem sitzt er lieber
> als einst am Totenbett.
> Er spukt durchs letzte Fieber
> Der Kerl in Violett.

> (The bed he loves to sit at
> Is a bed of death.
> The man in violet
> Haunts your final breath.)
> [Translated by E. Bentley]

Whether mocking, lamenting, or renouncing, the voice of the young poet is directed against those who try to avert man's attention from the misery (and glory) of this world and wish to console him with a better afterworld. He preaches instead:

> Lasst euch nicht verführen!
> Zu Frohn und Ausgezehr!
> Was kann euch Angst noch rühren?
> Ihr sterbt mit allen Tieren
> Und es kommt nichts nachher.

> (Don't let them lure you into
> Exhaustion and duress!
> Why all the trepidation?
> You die like all creation.
> And after: nothingness.)
> [Translated by E. Bentley]

It should be added that a division of Brecht's early poems into three thematic groups is both simplistic and also to some extent arbitrary. It leaves out, for instance, one of the most beautiful love poems Brecht ever wrote. "Erinnerung an die Marie A." (Memory of Marie A.) is based on a Breton lay of Marie de France (*ca.* 1100) which, in turn, became the model for Ezra Pound's "La Fraisne" of 1909. Brecht used for his version a rather vulgar popular World War I song which, according to the playwright Carl Zuckmayer, he succeeded in transforming into a genuine folk song.[7] This is not a true love poem but rather a poem about nature, in which a white cloud sparks the memory of a girl the poet once kissed under a plum tree. Her face and fate are now forgotten, but it is the image of the cloud that is still in his mind:

> Und auch den Kuss, ich hätt' ihn längst vergessen
> Wenn nicht die Wolke da gewesen wär
> Die weiss ich noch und werd ich immer wissen
> Sie war sehr weiss und kam von oben her.

> (Even the kiss would have been long forgotten
> If that white cloud had not been in the sky.
> I know the cloud, and shall know it forever,
> It was pure white and, oh, so very high.)
> [Translated by E. Bentley]

In addition to this unexpectedly tender and formally perfect poem at least one other, which also does not quite fit into the three groups outlined above, ought to be singled out, the "Chorale of the Man Baal," because it best exemplifies both the philosophy and tone of Brecht's first lyrical phase. Here it is the stark hammering rhythm, suggestive of the young poet's extraordinary power and his hunger for life, which gives the poem its almost hypnotic appeal from the very first lines, "Als im weissen Mutterschosse aufwuchs Baal" (When inside the white maternal womb grew Baal), to the end, when the dead Baal rots beneath the earth:

> War der Himmel noch so gross und still und fahl
> Jung und nackt und ungeheuer wunderbar
> Wie ihn Baal einst liebte, als Baal war.

(Large as ever was the sky and still and pale
Young and naked and almost miraculous
As Baal used to love it when Baal was.)
[Translated by E. Bentley]

In 1927, when *Die Hauspostille* appeared, German poetry
was highly individualistic, refined, sophisticated, aristocratic,
and generally withdrawn from the profane business of everyday life. The recognized masters were Stefan George, Hugo von
Hofmannsthal, and Rainer Maria Rilke, and the latter's widely
read *Das Stundenbuch* (Book of Hours) had initiated a tendency
toward writing lyrical prayers, so to speak. The new fashion was
also imitated by the Expressionists, and since Brecht scorned
their soul-baring efforts as well as poetry he felt was too personal and esoteric, he may deliberately have set out to do the
opposite in his first collection of verse. This accounts for his
choice of the ballad, the least individualized genre of lyrical
expression, the folk-song quality of his poetry, and the mocking
parodistic tone of the introductory "Guide to the Use of the
Individual Lessons." In a retrospective assessment of his lyrical
beginnings, Brecht stated:

In almost every genre I started conventionally. In poetry I began
with songs accompanied by the guitar and composed the verses
simultaneously with the music; the ballad was an ancient form and
in my time nobody who wanted to be somebody wrote ballads any-
more. Later I changed to other and less old forms, but I reverted
from time to time, even making copies of old masters and translating
Villon and Kipling. The type of song which came to this continent
after the war like a folk song of the big cities already had developed
a conventional form when I used it. I started with it and later
went beyond it.[8]

Notwithstanding the strongly parodistic element in *Die Hauspostille,* these words show an unexpected respect for tradition on
the part of the young rebel poet, because without mastery of,
and familiarity with, the old forms, nobody would or could
attempt parodies. In short, the poet Brecht was neither an in-
ventor of new lyrical forms nor an explorer of as yet unprobed
levels of consciousness. If his first book of verse nevertheless

charmed, enthralled, startled, electrified, stunned, and excited
unprofessional lovers of poetry as well as the most expert and
blasé literary critics, we must look for other qualities. These
are, first, an almost hypnotic rhythmic originality and, second,
a strongly sensual and concrete imagery combined with a rather
unique color typology. The sky may be mauve or "pale as
apricot" or drunk (starkly blue); and at night it "grows dark
like smoke," or the poet may sing of opal heavens and violet
horizons. A tree "sways like a drunk monkey," and the autumn
may bring "a day of blue September." Cities are black and their
inhabitants "black beasts of the pavements," while an old leaky
ship "vomits salt in remorse. It makes water in fear." Drunk-
ards have "lips of violet"; adventurers are "sick from the sun,
and gnawed at by the rainstorms," and a pirate "had hair like a
mole" while sailing through "absinthe seas." In *Die Hauspostille*,
Brecht broke through the thin veneer of the used-up German
literary language of his day and away from the highly intellectualized and introspective poetry of his contemporaries, associated
with the development of modern German literature and with
that of all other countries. It is this combination of stark language, metaphorical sensuality, and extraordinarily variegated
rhythm that caused Bentley to call the book "one of the best of
all books of modern poems."[9]

II *In the Service of Society*

While the first collection of verse by the young Brecht revealed
an outsider, a rebel, and an anarchist, who had composed his
ballads and songs in the meadows and under the trees of his
native town and had sung them to his friends in rural taverns, the
urbanizing influence of the big city of Berlin, which became his
new domicile in the early 1920's had a taming effect on him.
The difficult and tough conquest of Germany's theatrical capital
by the young man from the provinces coincided with the urban
orientation of the latest literary fashion: the new sobering
voices of Neo-Factualists replacing the ecstatic utterances of
the Expressionists. Partly preceding and partly coinciding with
the study of Marx, a new awareness of urbanization directed the
poet's attention to societal concern and responsibility, however

begrudging and reluctant at first. Significantly, Brecht gave to
the cycle of new poems written after *Die Hauspostille* the title
of *Lesebuch für Städtebewohner* (Reader for City Dwellers).
The poet's change of emphasis corresponds to the playwright's
shift from Baal's anarchic defiance to Galy Gay's adjustment to
life in the army and Garga's realization, at the end of *Im Dickicht
der Städte,* that "the chaos is used up now." The new city dweller,
while tough and cynical, is aware of the transitoriness of the
steel and concrete surrounding him and of the necessity to live
as cautiously as possible in order to avoid trouble. It is here
where the poet can help him. "Do not show your face," he
advises him, and "Do not open the door," and "He who was
not there and did not say anything, how can he be caught?"
Although Brecht, sobered-up, resigned, and cynical, was now far
removed from Baal's hymnic evocations of nature's bliss and
power, he equally welcomed the industrial environment and
singled out for his lyrical statement objects and experiences
of the man in the big city. There are songs about cranes for
coal mining, an ironical poem about the power of money, a
"memorial tablet" for twelve middleweight boxing champions,
a hymn to an oil tank, a poem in praise of automobiles, bitter
reflections on economic inequities and unemployment. After the
depression of 1929, the once highly praised and welcomed
example of America was conspicuously lamented in a long elegy
about "Verschollener Ruhm der Riesenstadt New York" (Forgotten Fame of the Giant City of New York). The new mood
and the new tone of the urban Brecht is perhaps best summed
up by the "Sang der Maschinen" (Song of the Machines), of
which the poet sings:

> Das ist kein Wind im Ahorn, mein Junge
> Das ist kein Lied an den einsamen Stern
> Das ist das wilde Geheul unserer täglichen Arbeit
> Wir verfluchen es und wir haben es gern
> Denn es ist die Stimme unserer Städte
> Es ist das Lied, das uns gefällt
> Es ist die Sprache, die wir alle verstehen
> Und bald ist es die Muttersprache der Welt.

(This is no wind in the maple-tree, my boy
This is no song to the lonely star
This is the wild howl of our daily labor
We curse it, yet we like it, too
For it is the voice of our cities
It is the song that pleases us
It is the language we all understand
And soon it will be the mother tongue of the world.)
[Translated by C. Hill]

While it would be an overstatement to ascribe these lines, and
similar poems written between 1926 and 1930, to a consciously
experienced social concern, they nevertheless reveal a new,
totally un-Baalian, tolerance of, and even solidarity with, the
insignificant little everyday urban man of today. The real impetus
for placing his poetic talent at the service of society came, of
course, from Brecht's simultaneous political involvement. His
didactic plays are full of poems which, even when removed
from their context, are often memorable for their power and
simplicity, such as "Lob des Lernens" ("Praise of Learning)
from *Die Mutter*, the middle part of which reads:

Such die Schule auf, Obdachloser!
Verschaffe dir Wissen, Frierender!
Hungriger, greif nach dem Buch: es ist eine Waffe.
Du musst die Führung übernehmen.

(Seek out the school, you who are homeless!
Sharpen your wits, you who shiver!
Hungry man, reach for the book: it is a weapon.
You must take over the leadership.)
[Translated by H. R. Hays]

Or the poet reveals his Marxist view when he raises, in "Fragen
eines lesenden Arbeiters" (A Worker Reads History), sly questions like: "Who built the seven gates of Thebes?" followed by
"Was it kings who hauled the craggy blocks of stone?" And after
many more irreverent questions he ends with the laconic statement: "Every ten years a great man, / who paid for the ex-
penses? / So many reports. / So many questions." In addition

to writing poems in free verse, Brecht also succeeded in com-
posing truly proletarian songs, set to music by Eisler and others
and intended to be sung by marching workers, such as "Keiner
oder Alle" (All of Us or None), which begins:

Sklave, wer wird dich befreien?
Die in tiefster Tiefe stehen
Werden, Kamerad, dich sehen
Und sie werden hör'n dein Schreien.
Sklaven werden dich befreien.

(Slave, who is it who shall free you?
Those in deepest darkness lying,
Comrade, these alone can see you,
They alone can hear you crying.
Comrade, only slaves can free you.)
[Translated by H. R. Hays]

Just as the fight against Hitler shifted the focus of Brecht's
drama from pro-Marxist *Lehrstücke* to antifascist plays, the poet
Brecht subordinated his lyrical talent to the active fight of Nazism,
and that to an even higher degree. If his antifascist poems considerably outnumber the pro-Marxist poems, the circumstances
of his life, and especially of his exile, are undoubtedly responsible. Brecht fought Hitler with his pen to the limits of his
capacity. His poems turned out to be powerful weapons, whether
published in countries adjacent to Germany, recited over the
radio by the BBC in London or by Radio Moscow, smuggled
across the border by partisan trucks, or dropped by Allied airplanes. Since writing *against* something results as much from
a sociopolitical motivation as fighting *for* a cause, we must consider Brecht's anti-Nazi poems part of a service to society that
could only be achieved at the expense of the poet's persona,
forced to remain mute until the hated foe had been defeated.
In a poem with the revealing title "Schlechte Zeit für Lyrik"
(Bad Times for Lyrics) he stated:

To use rhymes in my song
Would almost seem to be presumptuous.
Inside of me there is a struggle:

To be inspired by the blooming appletree
or horrified by the speeches of the paperhanger.
Only the second one
drives me to the writing desk.
[Translated by C. Hill]

And this, indeed, did happen on an unprecedented scale. Literally hundreds of poems owe their origin to Brecht's hatred of
Hitler and his regime—some of them mediocre, as most purely
topical writing often is, but many of them powerful and original
within the given limitations of political poetry. The elegy
"Deutschland" of 1933, for instance, is in the highest German
literary tradition, reminiscent of Friedrich Hölderlin, when it
begins:

> Oh Deutschland, bleiche Mutter!
> Wie sitzest du besudelt
> Unter den Völkern.
> Unter den Befleckten
> Fällst du auf.

> (O Germany, pale mother!
> How soiled you are
> As you sit among the peoples.
> You flaunt yourself
> Among the besmirched.)
> [Translated by H. R. Hays]

One of Brecht's finest ballads, the very long and touching "Kin-
derkreuzzug 1939" (Children's Crusade 1939) about a group of
Polish children, roaming through the war-torn countryside,
abandoned, and finally lost in a snowstorm, also owes its origin
to his war service with the pen. The stark simplicity Brecht
achieves here he also used with great effect in his so-called
"Hitler Chorales," a number of biting satirical poems composed
to the melodies of well-known Protestant church hymns in the
style first tried in *Die Hauspostille*. There are also numerous
other types of polemic poems, ranging from short epigrams to
ballads, soldier songs, chronicles, marching songs, satires, son-
nets, and long elegies. They show a poet whose societal con-

cern had imposed on him the conviction that "to speak of trees
is almost a crime, for it is a kind of silence about so many
horrors."[10]

III   *In the Company of the Classics*

Although Brecht possessed an extraordinary talent for rhyming (which does not come through in the English translations
of Bentley and Hays) and was equally at home in the traditional
simple four-line stanza, as well as in the more formal schemes
of the triplet and the sonnet, he tended more and more to a
special kind of free verse as he grew older. In an essay written in
1938, he explained that he came to his "Rhymeless Verse with
Irregular Rhythms" as a dramatist searching for an idiom suitable for showing "human dealings as contradictory, fiercely
fought over, full of violence."[11] Just as Brecht's theory of the
epic theater simultaneously developed with the discovery of
Marx, as we have seen, the newly sought poetic language had
to correspond to the discordances and inconsistencies in people's
social life. The oily smoothness of five-foot iambic meter, for
instance, would no longer do. It is here that the term gestus,
which we have explained earlier and which includes considerations of language, comes in. As Brecht formulated it: "The sentence must entirely follow the gestus of the person speaking,"
and "it seems to me at present that irregular rhythms must
further the gestic way of putting things."[12] What Brecht meant
may perhaps best be illustrated by another look at *Die heilige
Johanna der Schlachthöfe,* the plot of which follows the classical economic crisis in capitalistic society according to Marx,
as I mentioned in Chapter 3. We may now add that the language
of this first Brechtian poetic drama in the grand manner is
fashioned after the same societal principle: Joan's gestus demands the rhymeless verse with irregular rhythms that Brecht
was beginning to develop in those years. It is only logical that, as
the playwright Brecht became a sociopolitical writer, an *ecrivain
engagé*, the poet Brecht would also tend to abandon rhyme
and regular rhythm. It is for this reason that the bulk of his
lyrical output consists of free verse, which has found a wide following among younger German poets, while *Die Hauspostille*

has remained the unique testimony of a young anachronistic and inimitable genius.

Just as Marxism remained the firm philosophical basis of the mature and aging playwright, even after he had outgrown his rigid didactic and doctrinaire middle phase, so the irregular rhythm of Brecht's poetic voice, which he felt had to correspond to his notion of an erratic society, continued to dominate his profuse lyrical production. To this, however, we must add the increasing influence of a lifelong association with the classics.

Brecht's love for Latin goes back to his school days, as I pointed out in Chapter 1, and among the most frequently handled and annotated books in his library at the time of his death were editions of Latin classics, his special favorites being Horace and Lucretius. It was the figure of Coriolanus that caused the playwright Brecht to attempt a complete adaptation (really a new version) of Shakespeare's drama; it was the Roman general Lucullus who became the focal hero of a radio play and opera; and it was Brecht's interest in Caesar that made him write one of his very few novels, *Die Geschäfte des Herrn Julius Cäsar* (The Business Deals of Mr. Julius Caesar). His admiration for the great Latin poets sparked one of the strangest projects in the history of versification: a long-considered free recasting of the *Communist Manifesto* in hexameters, which grew to about four hundred lines before he gave it up in 1945. In itself it was to be only the second part of a long didactic poem modeled after Lucretius' *De Rerum Natura* with the tentative titles of "Lehrgedicht von der Natur der Menschen" (The Didactic Poem on the Nature of Man) or "Über die Unnatur der bürgerlichen Verhältnisse" (On the Nonnaturalness of Bourgeois Relations). Above all, however, it was Horace whom Brecht loved and who became one of his spiritual guides as the following short poem (1953) reveals :

> Even the Deluge
> Lasted not for ever.
> There came a time when
> The black waters stopped.
> Yet how few
> Lasted longer!
> [Translated by C. Hill]

Lifelong influences and habits are likely to leave a trace, and when a dead language like Latin was—and to some extent still is—retained in the curricula of European high schools to inculcate in pupils a sense of logic and orderliness and to improve their grasp of grammar, a poet with a similar indoctrination is bound to show the latinizing effect upon his style. In addition to the frequent use of the imperative and the question mark so characteristic of the teacher's role that the older Brecht appeared to assume increasingly in his poetry, his striking (and relatively non-German) preference for the present participle is undoubtedly derived from the structure of Latin grammar. Brecht himself made joking reference to it when he said: "The present participle should only be used by a person who had, as I did, a 'I' in Latin."[13] As the German scholar Walter Jens correctly pointed out, the employment of the present participle instead of a subordinating clause customary in German and introduced by the appropriate conjunction presupposes an intelligent reader, because it is he who will have to decide whether an adversative, a causal, or a temporal meaning is intended.[14]

Brecht did not only keep company with his beloved Latin classics but also deliberately learned from Oriental models. The playwright had already benefited from Japanese No-plays in his didactic phase; the theorist had observed the style of Chinese acting before he formulated his estrangement effect; now the poet's growing interest in Chinese philosophy and literature also enriched the colors on his lyrical palette. Lao-Tze, for instance, is the central character in one of Brecht's finest ballads, dealing with the transmission of politically useful knowledge, a subject doubly dear to him after he had personally experienced censorship and sealed borders.[15] Ten years later, while back in Berlin (1949), he still felt provoked to wrestle with Chinese poetry; this time it was Mao Tse-tung's "Thoughts while Flying over the Great Wall" that he tried to render into German. If one tries to assess the effect of Brecht's old-age love for things Chinese in general, and poets in particular, upon his own lyrical style, two things seem to stand out. On a philosophical level, the ideals he strives for and praises in his poems have become qualities of restraint, mellowness, and self-discipline, such as wisdom, goodness, friendliness, and politeness. On the level of language, a new austerity, shunning excessive word-age and attributive richness while avoiding the aridity of the earlier didactic phase, can be felt in Brecht's poetry of his third and most mature period, and by no means only in the lyrics specifically concerned with Chinese topics or models. New poems for children, a few new love poems, and a new type of very brief, epigrammatic, didactic verse also testify to Brecht's finally reached posture of a classic poet who has succeeded in compressing a maximum of meaning into a minimum of words.

Brevity alone is not a sign of high quality unless it is augmented by other evidence of formal mastery. In the case of Brecht, it is his unique ability to condense and contract lines and phrases in such a way that the reader's intelligence will have to supply the logical conclusions through his own substitution of missing words and thoughts. An epigrammatic poem of 1940 may serve as an example:

> From the library halls
> Emerge the butchers.
> Pressing the children to their sides
> The mothers stand and full of horror search
> The sky for the inventions of the scholars.
> [Translated by C. Hill]

Only when we realize that the scholars who come out of the library will have become the inventors and designers of bombs and missiles for which the mothers are searching the sky in times of war do we understand the poem and, thus, retroactively grasp the otherwise unintelligible second line. Or a charming children's song of 1952 retells the German legend of a tailor who jumped to his death from the steeple of Ulm cathedral with self-made wings because, as each of the two stanzas states "No one will ever fly, / The Bishop said to the people." This time it is the reader who will have to write his own third stanza, as it were, in order to conclude that (1) the tailor crashed because the wings were inadequate, and (2) the bishop was wrong, and man will eventually learn to fly.[16] Most of the characteristics we have just discussed, such as brevity, utmost simplicity, irregular rhythm, the ability to elicit an intellectual response by a technique of contracting, a distant and cool temperament, a measure of contentment, a longing for friendliness, can be found in Brecht's last small cycle of poems, which he wrote and published under the title *Buckower Elegien* (The Buckow Elegies) in 1953.[17] Nature, banned during the middle years of polemic writing, is now readmitted to his lyrical world; but instead of being a threatening and all-devouring danger to man, as it appeared to Baal, it is now domesticated and only seen in terms of its functional value for man. A flower garden is praised because ingeniously selected planting provides for continuous bloom from March until October; it makes the poet wish that "I, too, in good weather and bad, may show this or that which is pleasant." Nature without relation to human civilization is no longer of any interest. Observing smoke rising from the chimney of a little house on the lake, Brecht makes the significant comment that "if it were missing / how wretched then would be / the house and trees and lake." The poet has gone full circle; the shrill lament of anarchy has been subdued to the muted song of civilization; Baal has become Horace.

If we look back to Brecht's beginnings, follow the full range of his lyrical statements, and compare him with his contemporaries, we can now conclude that he occupies a rather exceptional place in his own native literature. While the traditional development of a German poet starts with an appreciation of Greek culture, continues along the milestones of Goethe and Schiller and the Romantic movement, and finally leads—mainly by way of Nietzsche and the French Symbolists—to an extremely individualistic and intellectualized lyrical idiom, Brecht's preference for Roman civilization, his love for Anglo-Saxon writers and places, his Chinese orientation resulting in a conscious adoption of aloofness and ceremonial politeness place him outside of the mainstream. I cannot agree with H. R. Hays when he states: "His genius for absorption is phenomenal and yet, at bottom, he is a traditional German poet still keeping alive the spirit of Heine."[18] While it is true that the early Brecht, like Heine, frequently used folk songs for his own adaptations and also came to the same painful rejection of the German Romantic spirit, Hays ought to know that it is precisely such a similarity that would exclude Brecht from being "a traditional German poet." It is a fact that Heine has remained suspect to German professors for political as well as racial reasons until today—witness the recent decision by the civic leaders of his native Düsseldorf *not* to name the new university after him. Brecht and Heine are the only two first-rate German poets who were also politically motivated to a high degree; they even shared the rare distinction of paying for their convictions with the hardship of exile abroad.

Looking beyond Brecht's native bonds and trying to assess his poetry from the perspective of world literature, we find that his very extensive, politically inspired verse-making makes him just as unique as he appeared to his countrymen. With few exceptions, the voice of the modern poet is highly personal and individualistic, generally sophisticated and intellectual, often metaphysical and esoteric. This is as true of the non-Germans Valéry, Eliot, Pound, Pasternak, E. E. Cummings, Auden, and many others, as it is of Hofmannsthal, George, Rilke, and Benn in Austria and Germany. Therefore, I agree with Hays when he continues: "Brecht is almost the only social poet writing today, the only social poet whose form and matter coincide, the only political poet in the proper sense of the word."[19] Commenting on the songs Brecht composed, either to his own tunes or set to music by renowned composers like Weill and Eisler, and sung by marching workers in many countries, Hays sums up Brecht's extraordinary contribution by adding: "They have enjoyed a popularity nothing short of amazing in an age in which poetry has tended to become more and more the concern of a few specialists."

There is another quality which, in my opinion, distinguishes Brecht's poetry from most other modern writers; it is to some extent already implicit in what was just stated. I am referring to his concept of functional poetry, first observed in the introduction to *Die Hauspostille* and symbolizing the subordination of the poet's persona to a higher purpose. This tendency, at first only mockingly admitted under the disguise of parody, gradually became stronger and more deliberate. It betrays a willingness to suppress the idiosyncrasies of the ego, a conscious effort to curb the excesses of bourgeois individualism which are felt to become obsolete in the expected and hoped-for times to come.

The adoption of rhymeless verse with irregular rhythms by an eminently musical poet who possessed a natural facility for easy rhyming; the relentless search for a neoclassic style devoid of purely decorative wordage; the self-denial of metaphoric richness and linguistic beauty by a master of the German tongue without contemporary equal; epigrammatic conciseness achieved by a new thought-compressing technique; the deliberate avoidance of the purely personal and autobiographical as he grew older—all these characteristics of Brecht's mature verse make him a unique phenomenon in contemporary world literature. He is the first consciously and intentionally nonindividualistic poet of our time. Future historians will have to decide whether this label will make Brecht the iconoclastic outsider in a highly individualistic and bourgeois tradition or the pioneering genius of a less individualistic future age with a more collective consciousness. Nobody, however, will deny that he was always motivated by deepest societal concerns and wielded his pen with the strength of moral conviction and extraordinary poetic inspiration. With more of his work becoming available in translation, Willett's prediction is likely to become true: "This may well be the most surprising thing of all for the English-language reader: to find that Brecht, whom Anglo-Saxons have been brought up to think of as a rather limited writer, has such a thoroughly equipped verse workshop under his hat."[20] As is to be expected, it was the master himself who best characterized the desired effect of his poetry with a few lines of utmost simplicity. Contemplating a picture of dried roots of Chinese tea plants which resembled the shape of a lion, Brecht wrote, three years before his death:

> The bad ones are fearful of your claws.
> The good ones are delighted with your charm.
> Something like this
> I would like to be said
> Of my own verse.
>
> [Translated by C. Hill]

CHAPTER 8

An Epitaph: Three Cheers for Brecht

O N the occasion of George Bernard Shaw's seventieth birth-
day, Brecht wrote a newspaper article entitled "Ovation
für Shaw." In an almost uncanny way, the young playwright,
who had then not yet embraced Marxism, eulogized the revered
British author in words that may serve as a fitting epitaph
for himself:

Shaw has applied a great part of his talent to intimidating people
to a point when it would be an impertinence for them to prostrate
themselves before him.

It will have been observed that Shaw is a terrorist. Shaw's brand of
terror is an extraordinary one, and he uses an extraordinary weapon,
that of humor. This extraordinary man seems to be of the opinion
that nothing in the world need be feared so much as the ordinary
man's calm and incorruptible eye, but that this must be feared
without question. This theory is for him the source of a great natural
superiority, and by applying it systematically he has ensured that
nobody who comes across him, in print, on the stage or in the flesh,
can conceive for a moment of his undertaking an action or speaking a
sentence without being afraid of that incorruptible eye. Indeed, even
the younger generation, whose qualifications lie largely in their aggressiveness, limit their aggressions to a strict minimum when they
realize that any attack on one of Shaw's habits, even his habit of
wearing peculiar underwear, is likely to end in the disastrous down-
fall of their own ill-considered garb.[1]

We do not know if the young Brecht was thinking of his own
habit of wearing silk shirts under his customary proletarian
jacket when he wrote these lines, but he came close to formulat-
ing the blueprint for creating his own notable stage figures
more than a decade later, when he continued:

181

Probably every single feature of all Shaw's characters can be attributed to his delight in dislocating our stock associations. He knows that we have a horrible way of taking all the characteristics of a particular type and lumping them under a single head. We picture a usurer as cowardly, furtive and brutal. Not for a moment do we think of allowing him to be in any way courageous. Or wistful, or tender-hearted. Shaw does.

As for the hero, Shaw's less gifted successors have developed his refreshing view that heroes are not models of good conduct and that heroism consists of an impenetrable but exceedingly lively hotchpotch of the most contradictory qualities; they have arrived at the lamentable conclusion that there is no such thing as either heroism or heroes. Probably in Shaw's view this is unimportant. He seems to find less point in living among heroes than among ordinary men.

Or let us consider the following tributes to Shaw in view of Brecht's own work and the criticism of his detractors:

It was clear to him that any decent man's working equipment had to include that vital piece of apparatus, his own trumpet. He proudly refuses to bury his pound sterling. . . . He knows just how much courage is needed to laugh at what is amusing, and how much seriousness to pick it out. . . . As a playwright he takes just as naive a view of writing for the theatre as young writers do, and he shows not the least trace of wishing to behave as if he ignored the fact; he makes free use of such naivety. . . . He said that in future people would no longer go to the theatre in order to understand something. What he probably meant was that, odd as it may seem, the mere reproduction of reality does not give an impression of truth. . . . Reading his works may not induce bacchic intoxication, but there is no doubt that it is extraordinarily healthy.

While it is astounding that Shaw's influence on Brecht has so far escaped the attention of critics and scholars it so richly deserves, it again points up the many paradoxes surrounding Brecht which we encountered in examining his life and work.[2] To begin with, after 1926 he mentioned Shaw as little as his subsequent renegade Marxist teachers Sternberg and Korsch, although both his aesthetics and his politics owe much to all three of them. Shaw's penchant for long introductions, comments, and essayistic writing in general repeats itself in Brecht's oeuvre, and there are still more similarities: both were socialists, both were great dramatists with epic tendencies but relatively poor novelists, both possessed sharp wit and epigrammatic brilliance. Willett's observation that Brecht ought to be more readily accepted by Anglo-Saxons because he often used English models comes to mind,[3] and yet it is another paradoxical fact that neither the poet nor the dramatist has fared well in the English-speaking countries, while it is precisely Brecht's Anglo-Saxon orientation that has separated him from the main literary tradition of his own native country. The man who, through his genius for clear thought and lucid style, was able to overcome the modern split between highbrow and lowbrow art and should, therefore, appeal to every theatergoer and reader, has paradoxically become the object of narrow intellectual as well as political cultism. The poet who invented his own new "rhymeless verse with irregular rhythms" turned out to be, upon objective consideration of his total output, unacceptable by, and without influence upon, the lyrical avant-garde of our time, but rather close to the conservative masters of modern poetry and consciously following the models of the classics. The theorist of an epic theater got stuck with a label he did not invent and wished to abandon at the end, while his aversion against mind-dulling and action-killing illusion has been widely misinterpreted and today lives in the minds of most people as an arid stage misuse without emotions. And yet, the same Brecht must be considered one of the most popular, recited and sung, politically influential poets of this century, while Brecht, the man of the theater, who was one of the most effective and inventive directors, is currently the most frequently produced playwright throughout the world. Paradoxes upon paradoxes! Only time will resolve them after the dramatist and the poet have survived the theoreticians and the cultists, as well as his political friends and enemies.

In the meantime, borrowing Willett's translation of "three cheers" for Brecht's "ovation for Shaw" of 1926, I should like to conclude this book with a tribute to Brecht as he appears to me in the year 1975:

Cheers to the first and only truly dialectical writer, possessed of burning social concern, aware of the overriding impact of science upon modern man, and trying to preserve the theater as a relevant and enjoyable institution in the twentieth century!

Cheers to the playwright who, endowed with the gift of creating unforgettable characters and blessed with unique powers of linguistic expression, was able to rescue and revive poetic drama in our time!

Cheers to the author whose work radiates, above all else, the rare quality of charm and the needed elixir of humor! Of the Brecht scholars it was Bentley who knew him better than most and who observed: "Only the most egregious art-snob or the blindest art-theorist can overlook the role of charm in art.... Another of the open secrets of Brecht was that while he attacked other forms of charm he had his own."[4] As to humor, the dramatist who in vain called on his audiences to "change the world: it needs it!"[5] may often have reconciled himself, in hours of doubt and disappointment, with the following variation of his famous line, which he took to heart: "Humor the world: it needs it!"

Notes and References

The most complete edition of Brecht's works as of today is a so-called Werkausgabe, *Gesammelte Werke* (Frankfurt: Suhrkamp, 1967). All references to it on the following pages are noted as *GW*.

Chapter One

1. Except the work notes of the last eighteen years of his life under the title *Arbeitsjournal* (Frankfurt: Suhrkamp, 1973).

2. From the autobiographical poem "Vom armen B.B." (Concerning Poor B.B.) written in 1922. *Selected Poems*, translated by H. R. Hays (New York: Grove Press, 1959), p. 15.

3. The so-called Gymnasium especially, with its heavy emphasis on the classics, has become a widely exploited literary target. Frank Wedekind's first play, *Spring's Awakening* (1891), for instance, drew its inspiration from a suicide wave in German high schools which even led to a parliamentary inquiry. Gerhart Hauptmann, Heinrich and Thomas Mann, Herman Hesse, and many other writers have conspicuously recorded their unpleasant experiences.

4. In a letter to the critic H. Ihering, published in the periodical *Sinn und Form*, first special Brecht issue (1945), p. 31.

5. Title of a book by the British scholar E. M. Butler (London, 1935).

6. Sergei Tretyakov, "Bert Brecht," in *International Literature*, Moscow (May, 1937). Reprinted in English by M. Esslin, *Brecht* (New York: Anchor Books, 1961), p. 7.

7. O. Münsterer, *Bert Brecht: Erinnerungen aus den Jahren 1917–1922* (Zürich: Verlag der Arche, 1963), pp. 94–98.

8. B. Reich, "Erinnerungen an den jungen Brecht," *Sinn und Form*, second Brecht issue (1957), p. 432. Reprinted in English by M. Esslin, *op. cit.*, p. 18.

9. See note 2 above.

10. Lion Feuchtwanger, "Bertolt Brecht (Dargestellt für Engländer)," *Die Weltbühne*, Berlin (September 4, 1928); also in *Sinn und Form*, second Brecht issue (1957), pp. 107–108. My translation.

11. See notes 2 and 9 above.

12. Carl Zuckmayer, *Als wär's ein Stück von mir* (Frankfurt: S. Fischer, 1971), p. 380.

13. Willy Haas, *Bert Brecht* (Berlin: Colloquium, 1958), p. 6.

14. Rudolf Frank, "Brecht von Anfang," in *Das Ärgernis Brecht*, (Basel: Basilius-Presse, 1961), p. 34.

15. Fritz Sternberg, *Der Dichter und die Ratio* (Göttingen: Sachse & Pohl, 1963), p. 12, pp. 22–25.

16. Brecht, *Prosa*, Volume II (Frankfurt: Suhrkamp, 1965), pp. 120–121. My translation.

17. Brecht, *Flüchtlingsgespräche* (Conversations among Refugees), published after Brecht's death in *Prosa*, Volume II, p. 151. My translation.

18. The historical-critical edition of Brecht's works, including all fragments and workbooks, originally planned with the assistance of the East German Academy, will not be forthcoming for some time. As long as the numerous and often overlapping volumes, including the *Werkausgabe* of 1967, are doing as well as they apparently do, a definitive edition is not likely to appear. Thus, it would seem that both political and commercial reasons prolong the tentative phase of Brecht scholarship.

19. The deliberately stylized semilegendary Russia in the opening scene of *Der Kaukasische Kreidekreis* is obviously no refutation of this statement.

20. From the long autobiographical poem "An die Nachgeborenen" (To Posterity) of 1938. *Selected Poems* (New York: Grove Press, 1959), p. 175.

Chapter Two

1. O. Münsterer, *Brecht: Erinnerungen aus den Jahren 1917–22* (Zürich: Verlag der Arche, 1963), pp. 21–25, 109–117.

2. A facetious allusion to the hero of Kafka's *The Trial* is suggested by Hugo Schmidt, who provided the notes to Bentley's American edition of *Die Hauspostille* [Manual of Piety] (New York: Grove Press, 1966), p. 307. If true, it would tend to corroborate my speculation about Kafka's influence on Brecht's *Im Dickicht der Städte*; compare note 7 below.

3. Quoted from the translation in *The Tulane Drama Review* (Autumn, 1961), p. 114.

4. O. Münsterer, *op. cit.*, pp. 87–89.

5. A. Bronnen, *Tage mit Bertolt Brecht* (Munich: Kurt Desch, 1960), pp. 47–48.

6. O. Münsterer, *op. cit.*, p. 151.

7. W. Benjamin and W. Mittenzwei have established Brecht's interest in Kafka, but date its beginning as late as 1931 on the basis of verifiable notes, references, and conversations. I am still convinced that Kafka's influence had already manifested itself a decade earlier. Compare also note 2 above.

8. Brecht, *Collected Plays*, Volume I (New York: Vintage Books, 1971), p. 423.

9. *Ibid.*, p. 421.

10. Brecht, *Stücke*, Volume II (Frankfurt: Suhrkamp, 1957), pp. 235–236. My translation.

11. John Willett, ed. and trans., *Brecht on Theatre* (New York: Hill & Wang, 1964), p. 43.

12. A. Bronnen, *op. cit.*, p. 143.

Chapter Three

1. In view of Lindbergh's pro-Nazi views Brecht later omitted his name, changed the title to *Ozeanflug* (Ocean Flight), wrote a new prologue, and excluded the play from the subsequent edition of his collected plays.

2. Fritz Sternberg, *Der Dichter und die Ratio* (Göttingen: Sachse & Pohl, 1963), pp. 12, 16.

3. See also the quotation at the end of Chapter 1 on p. 39.

4. According to Hochhuth, Churchill acquiesced in the assassination of General Sikorsky, the head of the Polish Government in Exile, in order not to jeopardize the more important British-Russian alliance against Hitler.

5. Käthe Rülicke, "Die heilige Johanna" in *Sinn und Form*, X (1959), pp. 429–444.

6. Ronald Gray, *Brecht* (Edinburgh: Oliver & Boyd, 1961), p. 53.

7. Fritz Sternberg, *op. cit.*, pp. 24–26.

8. "On Rhymeless Verse with Irregular Rhythms," in John Willett, *Brecht on Theatre*, pp. 115–120.

9. Compare note 7 above.

10. A full, and often hilarious, account is presented by Lee Baxandall, "Brecht in America, 1935," *The Drama Review* XII (1967). Reprinted in *Brecht*, ed. E. Munk (New York: Bantam Books, 1972), pp. 36–60.

11. With the only exception of a student production at Harvard University in 1971, as far as I can ascertain. Translation by Leonard J. Lehrman.

12. H. Kaufmann, *Bertolt Brecht: Geschichtsdrama und Parabelstück* (Berlin: Rütten & Löning, 1962), p. 46.

Chapter Four

1. Reprinted in *Brecht*, ed. P. Demetz (Englewood Cliffs, N.J.: Prentice Hall, 1962), p. 33.

2. In the meantime, Suhrkamp has commissioned a volume containing background materials and versions of the play; it was not yet available at the time of the writing of this book.

3. In a conversation with Ernst Schumacher, reported in *Erinnerungen an Brecht*, ed. H. Witt (Leipzig: Reclam, 1967), p. 336.

4. F. Ewen, *Bertolt Brecht* (New York:: Citadel Press, 1967), p. 307.

5. M. Esslin, *Brecht*, p. 175.

6. Brecht, *Stücke*, Volume IX (Berlin: Suhrkamp, 1957), p. 369. My translation.

7. My translation.

8. Quoted in English by F. Ewen, *op. cit.*, p. 407.

9. Fritz Sternberg, *Der Dichter und die Ratio*, pp. 13–14. My translation.

Chapter Five

1. *Simplicius Simplicissimus* or *The Adventurous Simplicissimus* (1669), the first and extremely successful apprenticeship novel by Hans Jakob Christoffel von Grimmelshausen (1610 or 1625 to 1676), was followed by several minor novels, the first of which is *The Runagate Courage* (1670).

2. Compare Chapter 3, pp. 67–70.

3. Hans Bunge, *Fragen Sie mehr über Brecht: Hanns Eisler im Gespräch* (Munich: Rogner & Bernhard, 1970), p. 228.

4. See also under "V effect" in Chapter 6, pp. 146–47, 151.

5. *Seven Plays by Bertolt Brecht*, ed. Eric Bentley (New York: Grove Press, 1961), p. xlii.

6. John Willett, *The Theatre of Bertolt Brecht* (New York: New Directions, 3rd revised edition, 1968), p. 103.

7. Ernst Schumacher, *Drama und Geschichte: Bertolt Brechts "Leben des Galilei" und andere Stücke* (Berlin: Rütten & Löning, 1968), and Werner Mittenzwei, *Brecht: Von der "Massnahme" zu "Leben des Galilei"* (Berlin: Aufbau-Verlag, 1962).

8. Gerhard Szczesny, *The Case against Bertolt Brecht* [translated from the German] (New York: Frederick Ungar, 1969), especially pp. 45–60, where the author attempts a demolition of Brecht's character from a layman's psychoanalytical point of view.

9. *GW*, XVII (*Schriften zum Theater 3*), p. 1106.

Notes and References

10. *GW*, XVIII (*Schriften zur Literatur und Kunst 1*), p. 222.

11. Ernst Schumacher, *Bertolt Brechts "Leben des Galilei"* (Berlin: Henschelverlag, 1965), p. 113.

12. *GW*, XVII (*Schriften zum Theater 3*), p. 1133.

13. Bentley in *Seven Plays by Bertolt Brecht*, p. xxiv.

14. Hans Bunge, *Fragen Sie mehr über Brecht: Hanns Eisler im Gespräch* p. 254.

15. Brecht, *Arbeitsjournal* (Frankfurt: Suhrkamp-Verlag, 1973), p. 45. My translation.

16. *Ibid.*, p. 52.

17. Walter H. Sokel, "Brecht's Split Characters and His Sense of the Tragic," in *Brecht*, ed. Peter Demetz (Englewood Cliffs, N.J.: Prentice-Hall, 1962), p. 129.

18. *Arbeitsjournal*, p. 171.

19. Ralph Ley, "Compassion and Absurdity: Brecht and Marx on the Truly Human Community," in *Studies in German Literature of the Nineteenth and Twentieth Centuries*, ed. Siegfried Mews (Chapel Hill: University of North Carolina Press, 1970), pp. 223–235.

20. *Ibid.*, p. 227.

21. Jost Hermand, "Herr Puntila und sein Knecht Matti" in *Brecht Heute—Brecht Today*, Jahrbuch der internationalen Brecht-Gesellschaft, I (1971), p. 125.

22. Martin Esslin, *Brecht*, p 306.

23. Claude Hill, "Bertolt Brecht," in *Symposium*, XV, 4 (1961), p. 261.

24. *The Caucasian Chalk Circle*, revised English version by Eric Bentley (New York: Grove Press, 1966), pp. 10–11.

25. Ronald Gray, *Brecht* (Edinburgh: Oliver and Boyd, 1961), p. 105.

26. See also notes 19 and 20 above.

27. Bentley in *Seven Plays by Bertolt Brecht*, p. xlviii.

28. John Fuegi, "The Caucasian Chalk Circle in Performance," in *Brecht Heute—Brecht Today*, I (1971), p. 140.

29. John Fuegi in the same article, pp. 146–148; to a lesser extent, Charles R. Lyons in his *Bertolt Brecht: The Despair and the Polemic* (Carbondale: Southern Illinois University Press, 1968), pp. 147–148.

30. Manfred Wekwerth, "Auffinden einer aesthetischen Kategorie," in *Sinn und Form*, second Brecht issue (1957); reprinted in *Erinnerungen an Brecht* (Leipzig: Reclam, 1964). Wekwerth quotes Brecht, shortly before his death, as stating that "the naïve is the most concrete aesthetic category."

Chapter Six

1. John Willett, *The Theatre of Bertolt Brecht,* third revised edition (New York: New Directions, 1968), p. 165.

2. Brecht, "Notes on Erwin Strittmatter's play *Katzgraben,*" in John Willett, *Brecht on Theatre* (New York: Hill & Wang, 1964), pp. 247–248.

3. From a published letter by Fritz Sternberg to Brecht in the *Berliner Börsen-Courier* of June 2, 1927; quoted in Frederic Ewen's translation in his *Bertolt Brecht* (New York: The Citadel Press, 1967), p. 199.

4. Rudolf Frank, *Spielzeit meines Lebens* (Heidelberg: Lambert Schneider, 1960), p. 266; quoted in Ewen's translation, see above, p. 201.

5. John Willett, *The Theatre of Bertolt Brecht,* p. 173.

6. Kurt Weill, "Gestus in Music," *Die Musik* (1929); English version in *The Tulane Drama Review,* Volume VI, No. 1 (September, 1961).

7. In an essay, probably written in 1940 and translated by Willett in his *Brecht on Theatre,* p. 140.

8. Reported by the director Manfred Wekwerth from a visit to Brecht's country house in 1956, first published in *Sinn und Form,* second special Brecht issue (1957) and reprinted in *Erinnerungen an Brecht* (Leipzig: Reclam, 1964), pp. 221–223. See also Chapter 5, note 30.

9. Chart and footnote translated by me from the revised edition of 1938, published for the first time in *GW* XVII (1967), pp. 1109–10.

10. *GW,* XV, p. 70. My translation.

11. John Willett, *Brecht on Theatre,* p. 121.

12. *Ibid.,* p. 124.

13. *Ibid.,* paragraph 3 on p. 180, and paragraph 65, p. 200.

14. These quotations and additional evidence for Hegel's influence on Brecht's humor in Helmut Jendreiek, *Bertolt Brecht* (Düsseldorf: A. Bagel, 1969), pp. 67–71.

15. See note 8, *Erinnerungen an Brecht,* pp. 220–221.

16. *GW,* XV (*Schriften zum Theater 1*), p. 141.

17. *Ibid.,* p. 151.

18. From an article, unpublished during Brecht's life, in John Willett, *Brecht on Theatre,* p. 74.

19. Mordecai Gorelik, "Rational Theater," in *Brecht Heute,* Yearbook of the International Brecht-Society, I (1971), p. 54.

20. John Willett, *Brecht on Theatre,* p. 41.

21. Compare discussions of *Mahagonny* (Chapter 2), *Die*

Massnahme (Chapter 3), and *Der Gute Mensch von Sezuan* (Chapter 5).

22. This and the following quotation from *The Messingkauf Dialogues*, tr. John Willett (London: Methuen & Co., 1965), p. 105.

23. *Arbeitsjournal*, Volume II (Frankfurt: Suhrkamp, 1973), p. 837. My translation.

24. Ernst Schumacher, "Er wird bleiben," in *Erinnerungen an Brecht* (Leipzig: Reclam, 1964), p. 339. My translation.

Chapter Seven

1. John Willett was the major foreign Brecht scholar at a Brecht symposium, April 1–3, 1971, which I organized and hosted on the campus of Rutgers University. The revised and complete text of his talk on Brecht's poetry appeared in *Brecht Heute—Brecht Today*, Jahrbuch der Internationalen Brecht Gesellschaft II, (1972), pp. 88–104.

2. Brecht, *Manual of Piety*, bilingual edition, trans. Eric Bentley (New York: Grove Press, 1966), and Bertolt Brecht, *Selected Poems*, trans. H. R. Hays (New York: Grove Press, 1959), now a Harcourt Brace paperback.

3. This and the preceding quotation from Willy Haas, *Bertolt Brecht* (Berlin: Colloquium Verlag, 1958), p. 41. My translation.

4. Bentley in *Manual of Piety*, p. xi.

5. A more penetrating analysis of this poem, linking it with a similar "Moritat" by Wedekind and the use of the grotesque, is to be found in an article by Ulrich Weisstein in *The German Quarterly*, XLV (March, 1972), pp. 295–310.

6. Brecht got to know Rimbaud's poem "Le bateau ivre" through K. L. Ammer, who had translated it as "Das trunkene Schiff." Ammer's translation of Villon had inspired many songs of *Die Dreigroschenoper*. We have already encountered Rimbaud's influence in our discussion of *Baal* and *Im Dickicht der Städte*.

7. Carl Zuckmayer, *Als wär's ein Stück von mir* (Frankfurt: S. Fischer, 1971), p. 375.

8. Brecht, *Über Lyrik* (Frankfurt: edition Suhrkamp No. 70), p. 14. My translation.

9. Bentley in *Manual of Piety*, p. xi.

10. Brecht, lines 7 and 8 of the poem "An die Nachgeborenen," written in 1938. The poem is also quoted at the end of Chapter 1.

11. "On Rhymeless Verse with Irregular Rhythms," in John Willett, *Brecht on Theatre* (New York: Hill & Wang, 1964), p. 116.

12. *Ibid.*, p. 117.

13. Reported by Walter Jens in his edition of *Ausgewählte Gedichte* (Frankfurt: edition Suhrkamp No. 86, 1964), p. 89.

14. *Ibid.*

15. The complete translated title of this ballad, one of Brecht's finest, would read: "Legend about the Origin of the Book *Taoteking* on Lao-Tze's Road into Emigration."

16. The false statement by the bishop can also be seen as Brecht's application of the estrangement effect to his poetry: the startled reader must supply the correct conclusion.

17. The aging and ailing Brecht often relaxed and recuperated in his lakeside cottage in the suburban village of Buckow.

18. Brecht, *Selected Poems*, trans. H. R. Hays, p. 8.

19. *Ibid.*, p. 3.

20. John Willett, "The Poet beneath the Skin," in *Brecht Heute—Brecht Today*, II (1972), p. 103.

Chapter Eight

1. This passage and the following excerpts are taken from Brecht's article in the translation of John Willett under the title 'Three Cheers for Shaw" in *Brecht on Theatre* (New York: Hill & Wang, 1957), pp. 10–11.

2. I am aware of only one recent investigation: Karl A. Schoeps, *Bertolt Brecht and Bernard Shaw: Eine Untersuchung von Einflüssen und Parallelen.* Unpublished dissertation, Univ. of Wisconsin, 1971. The published version (Bonn: Bouvier Verlag Herbert Grundmann, 1974) was not available to me before the galleys of this book had already been corrected.

3. Willett gives the following examples: "He illustrated his opinions by citing Auden and Chaplin, Shelley and Swift, Hogarth and Low; he liked our traditional qualities of clarity and restraint. He worked, as we have seen, on Shakespeare and Marlowe, Webster, Farquhar, Gay, and Synge; he was an addict of the English and American detective story, taking much of the tone and style of the *Dreigroschenroman* from Edgar Wallace and *Arturo Ui* from the old gangster films." From John Willett, *The Theatre of Bertolt Brecht* (New York: New Directions, 3rd revised edition 1968), p. 217.

4. In the introduction to *Seven Plays by Bertolt Brecht* (New York: Grove Press, 1961), p. xiv.

5. From *Die Massnahme*, Scene 5.

Selected Bibliography

PRIMARY SOURCES

1. In German

The most complete edition of Brecht's works is *Gesammelte Werke* in twenty paperback volumes, Frankfurt: Suhrkamp, 1967 (listed as *GW* in the notes), also simultaneously published in eight thin-paper hardcover volumes and augmented in 1969 by a volume containing the film scripts. The following editions, published by Suhrkamp in Frankfurt and concurrently by Aufbau Verlag in East Berlin, are also still in print:

Stücke, 14 volumes, 1953–1967.
Gedichte, 9 volumes, 1960–1969.
Schriften zum Theater, 7 volumes, 1963–1964.
Prosa, 5 volumes, 1965 (only by Suhrkamp).
Schriften zur Literatur und Kunst, 3 volumes, 1966–1967.
Schriften zur Politik und Gesellschaft, 1 volume, 1968.
Texte für Filme, 2 volumes, 1969 (only by Suhrkamp).

Most of the major plays, as well as selections of poetry and miscellaneous writings, are also available in the small paperback volumes of the edition Suhrkamp series, complemented by volumes containing materials relating to the origin of and comments on specific plays. Started in 1963, some of these *Materialien zu . . .* have already appeared and some are still in various stages of preparation. The most important recent publication, not included in *GW*, is the *Arbeitsjournal* (Frankfurt: Suhrkamp, 1973), containing Brecht's work notes from 1938 until 1955 in two volumes plus notes.

2. In English

Seven Plays. Edited and with an introduction by Eric Bentley. New York: Grove Press, 1961.
Works. General editor, Eric Bentley. New York: Grove Press, since 1956 and still in progress. (Contains most major plays in small paperback volumes.)

Collected Plays. Edited by Ralph Manheim and John Willett. New
York: Random House, Vintage Books. Hardcover edition by
Pantheon Books. (In progress since 1971, with new translations
and editorial notes. Volumes I, V, and IX have appeared as of
this writing.)
Selected Poems. Translation and introduction by H. R. Hays. Bilingual
edition. New York: Harcourt Brace, 1947. A Harvest Book.
Manual of Piety. Bilingual edition with English text by Eric Bentley
and notes by H. Schmidt. New York: Grove Press, 1966.
The Threepenny Novel. Translated by D. L. Vesey and C. Isherwood.
New York: Grove Press, 1956.
Brecht on Theatre: The Development of an Aesthetic. Edited and
translated by John Willett. New York: Hill & Wang, 1964.
The Messingkauf Dialogues. Translated by John Willett. London:
Methuen & Co., 1965.

SECONDARY SOURCES

The quickly proliferating literature on Brecht is so vast that any
attempt at completeness would be beyond the scope of this book.
Therefore, I have limited myself to listing only books and articles
which would seem to be helpful to the general reader who is not a
Brecht specialist and to whom the *World Authors Series* is addressed.
For the benefit of those who can read German, materials in English
and in German have been listed separately. Sources of a specialized
nature dealing with individual works and narrow topics only, while
fully identified in the preceding section of Notes and References, are
not reintroduced here, nor are articles collected in books and special
Brecht issues of periodicals listed below. Treatments of, or substantial
comments on, specific major plays are to be found in the entries
marked by an asterisk.

1. Bibliographies

GRIMM, REINHOLD. *Bertolt Brecht.* Fourth edition. Stuttgart: Metzler,
1971.
HILL, CLAUDE, and RALPH LEY. *The Drama of German Expressionism.*
Chapel Hill: University of North Carolina Press, 1960, reprinted
by AMS Press, New York, 1966. Lists English translations of
Brecht's works and writings about him up to 1958.
NUBEL, WALTER. "Bertolt Brecht Bibliographie." *Sinn und Form,*
second special Brecht issue. Berlin: Rütten & Loening, 1957,
pp. 481–628.

PETERSEN, KLAUS-DIETRICH. "Bertolt Brecht Bibliographie." In *Bertolt Brecht: Leben und Werk*. Dortmund, 1966, pp. 35–143. Continues Nubel's bibliography from 1957 to 1964.

––––––. "Kommentierte Auswahlbibliographie." In *Text und Kritik, Sonderband Bertolt Brecht*. Munich: Richard Boorberg Verlag, 1972, pp. 142–158. Best and most recent selected bibilography in German.

SUVIN, D., M. SPALTER, and R. SCHOTTER. "A Selected Brecht Bibliography." In *The Drama Review*, Volume XII, No. 2 (T 38) (1968). Includes a discography of recordings of Brecht's works.

SUVIN, DARKO. "Brecht—An Essay at a Dramaturgic Bibliography." In *Brecht*, edited by Erika Munk. New York: Bantam Books, 1972. The most recent selected bibliography in English.

2. Books in German (including anthologies of writings on Brecht)

ANDERS, GUENTHER. *Bert Brecht: Gespräche und Erinnerungen*. Zürich: Verlag der Arche, 1962.

Das Ärgernis Brecht. Includes articles by S. Melchinger, R. Frank, R. Grimm, E. Franzen, O. Mann. Basel: Basilius Presse, 1961.

ARNOLD, H. L., ed. *Text + Kritik*. Special issue: Bertolt Brecht I. Munich: Richard Boorberg Verlag, 1972.

BENJAMIN, WALTER. *Versuche über Brecht*. Frankfurt: Suhrkamp (edition Suhrkamp 172), 1966.

Bertolt Brecht: Sein Leben und Werk. With contributions by W. Hecht, H. J. Bunge, K. Rülicke-Weiler. East Berlin, 1969.

BRONNEN, ARNOLT. *Tage mit Bertolt Brecht*. Munich: Kurt Desch Verlag, 1960.

BRÜGGEMANN, HEINZ. *Literarische Technik und soziale Revolution*. Versuche über das Verhältnis von Kunstproduktion, Marxismus und literarischer Tradition in den theoretischen Schriften Bertolt Brechts. Reinbeck bei Hamburg: Rowohlt, 1973.

BUNGE, HANS. *Fragen Sie mehr über Brecht: Hanns Eisler im Gespräch*. Munich: Rogner & Bernhard, 1970.

FASSMANN, KURT. *Brecht: Eine Bildbiographie*. Munich: Kindler Verlag, 1958.

GOEDHART, GERDA. *Bertolt Brecht Portraits*. Zürich: Verlag der Arche, 1964.

GRIMM, REINHOLD. *Bertolt Brecht: Die Struktur seines Werkes*. Nuremberg: Verlag Hans Carl, 1959.

––––––. *Brecht und die Weltliteratur*. Nuremberg: Verlag Hans Carl, 1961.

HAAS, WILLY. *Bert Brecht*. Berlin: Colloquium Verlag, 1958.

HECHT, WERNER, ed. *Brecht-Dialog 1968*. Politik auf dem Theater. Berlin: Henschelverlag, 1968.

——. *Brechts Weg zum epischen Theater*. Berlin: Henschelverlag, 1962.

HINCK, WALTER. *Die Dramaturgie des späten Brecht*. Göttingen: Vandenhoeck & Ruprecht, 1959.

HÖGEL, MAX. *Bertolt Brecht: Ein Portrait*. Augsburg: Verlag der schwäbischen Forschungsgemeinschaft, 1962.

HULTBERG, HELGE. *Die ästhetischen Anschauungen Bertolt Brechts*. Copenhagen: Munksgaard, 1962.

IHERING, HERBERT. *Bertolt Brecht und das Theater*. Berlin: Rembrandt-Verlag, 1959.

*JENDREIEK, HELMUT. *Bertolt Brecht*. Düsseldorf: August Bagel Verlag, 1969.

*KAUFMANN, HANS. *Bertolt Brecht: Geschichtsdrama und Parabelstück*. Berlin: Rütten & Loening, 1962.

KESTING, MARIANNE. *Bertolt Brecht in Selbstzeugnissen und Bilddokumenten*. Hamburg: Rowohlt, 1959.

KLOTZ, VOLKER. *Bertolt Brecht: Versuch über das Werk*. Darmstadt: Hermann Gentner, 1957.

MAYER, HANS. *Bertolt Brecht und die Tradition*. Pfullingen: Neske, 1961.

——. *Anmerkungen zu Brecht*. Frankfurt: Suhrkamp (edition Suhrkamp 143), 1965.

*MITTENZWEI, WERNER. *Bertolt Brecht: Von der "Massnahme" zu "Leben des Galilei."* Berlin: Aufbau-Verlag, 1962.

MÜLLER, ANDRÉ. *Kreuzzug gegen Brecht*. Darmstadt: Progress-Verlag, 1963.

MÜNSTERER, HANS OTTO. *Bert Brecht: Erinnerungen aus den Jahren 1917–22*. Zürich: Verlag der Arche, 1963.

*RISCHBIETER, HENNING. *Brecht I* and *Brecht II*. Velber bei Hannover: Friedrich Verlag, 1966. (Friedrichs Dramatiker des Welttheaters 13 and 14).

RÜLICKE-WEILER, KÄTHE. *Die Dramaturgie Brechts*. Berlin: Henschelverlag, 1966.

*SCHMIDT, DIETER. *"Baal" und der junge Brecht*. Stuttgart: Metzler, 1966.

SCHRIMPF, HANS JOACHIM. *Lessing und Brecht*. Pfullingen: Neske, 1965.

SCHUHMANN, KLAUS. *Der Lyriker Bertolt Brecht 1913–1933*. Berlin: Rütten & Loening, 1964.

*SCHUMACHER, ERNST. *Die dramatischen Versuche Bert Brechts 1918–1933*. Berlin: Rütten & Loening, 1955.

°————. *Bertolt Brechts "Leben des Galilei" und andere Stücke.* Berlin: Henschel, 1965.

————. *Brecht.* Theater und Gesellschaft im 20. Jahrhundert. 21 Aufsätze. Berlin: Henschel, 1973.

°*Sinn und Form.* First special Brecht issue, 1949, and second special Brecht issue, 1957. East Berlin: Rütten & Loening. The two volumes contain a wealth of material by scholars and critics from many countries.

STERNBERG, FRITZ. *Der Dichter und die Ratio.* Göttingen: Sachse & Pohl, 1963.

VÖLKER, KLAUS. *Brecht-Chronik.* Munich: Hanser, 1971.

Weimarer Beiträge. Special Brecht issue, 1968.

WEKWERTH, MANFRED. *Schriften. Arbeit mit Brecht.* Berlin: Henschel, 1973.

°WITT, HUBERT, ed. *Erinnerungen an Brecht.* Leipzig: Philipp Reclam, 1964. Contains reminiscences by L. Feuchtwanger, M. Frisch, Lotte Lenya, M. Wekwerth, E. Schumacher, and many others.

ZWERENZ, GERHARD. *Aristotelische und Brechtsche Dramatik.* Rudolstadt: Greifenverlag, 1956.

3. Books in English (including anthologies of writings on Brecht)

°*Brecht Heute—Brecht Today.* Vols. I (1971) and II (1972). Jahrbuch der internationalen Brecht-Gesellschaft, edited by G. Bahr, E. Bentley, J. Fuegi, R. Grimm, J. Hermand, W. Hinck, J. Spalek, U. Weisstein. Frankfurt: Athenäum-Verlag. Contains contributions in English and in German.

°DEMETZ, PETER, ed. *Brecht.* A collection of critical essays. Englewood Cliffs, N.J.: Prentice-Hall, 1962. Contains Brecht's testimony before the House Committee on Un-American Activities.

ESSLIN, MARTIN. *Brecht: The Man and His Work.* Garden City: Doubleday & Co. (Anchor Books), 1961.

°EWEN, FREDERIC. *Bertolt Brecht: His Life, His Art, and His Time.* New York: The Citadel Press, 1967.

°FUEGI, JOHN. *The Essential Brecht.* Los Angeles: Hennessey & Ingalls, 1972.

GRAY, RONALD. *Brecht.* Edinburgh and London: Oliver & Boyd, 1961.

°KNUST, HERBERT and SIEGFRIED MEWS, eds. *Essays on Brecht: Theater and Politics.* Chapel Hill: University of North Carolina Press, 1974.

°LYONS, CHARLES R. *Bertolt Brecht: The Despair and the Polemic.* Carbondale: Southern Illinois University Press, 1968.

*Munk, Erika, ed. *Brecht.* A selection of critical pieces from *The Drama Review.* New York: Bantam Books, 1972.

*Szczesny, Gerhard. *The Case against Bertolt Brecht.* New York: Frederick Ungar, 1969. (Translated from German.)

Weideli, Walter. *The Art of Bertolt Brecht.* New York: New York University Press, 1963. (Translated from French.)

Willett, John. *The Theatre of Bertolt Brecht.* New York: New Directions, 3rd revised edition, 1968.

4. Articles and Essays of a General Nature in German

Arendt, Hannah. "Der Dichter Bertolt Brecht." *Die Neue Rundschau,* 61 (1950), pp. 53–67.

————. "Quod licet Jovi . . . Reflexionen über den Dichter Bertolt Brecht und sein Verhältnis zur Politik." *Merkur,* 23 (1969), pp. 527–542, 625–642.

Brandt, Thomas. "Bertolt Brecht und sein Amerikabild." *Universitas,* 21 (1966), pp. 719–734.

Frisch, Max. "Brecht als Klassiker." *Dichten und Trachten* 6, Frankfurt (1955); also in *Die Weltwoche,* Zurich, July 1, 1955.

Grimm, Reinhold. "Bertolt Brecht." In *Deutsche Dichter der Moderne,* ed. Benno von Wiese. Berlin: Schmidt, 1965.

————. "Brechts letzte Handbibliothek." *Germanisch-Romanische Monatschrift,* 9 (1960), pp. 451–463.

Herzfelde, Wieland. "Der Lyriker Bertolt Brecht." *Aufbau,* 7 (1951), pp. 1097–1104.

Hill, Claude. "Bertolt Brecht." *Universitas,* 15 (December, 1960), pp. 1275–1288.

Holthusen, Hans Egon. "Versuch über Brecht." In his *Kritisches Verstehen.* Munich: Piper, 1961, pp. 7–137.

Jens, Walter. "Protokoll über Brecht: Ein Nekrolog." *Merkur,* 10 (1956), pp. 943–965.

————. "Poesie und Doktrin, Bertolt Brecht." In his *Statt einer Literaturgeschichte.* Pfullingen: Neske, 1957, pp. 227–258.

Lüthy, Herbert. "Vom armen Bert Brecht." *Der Monat,* 44 (1952), pp. 115–144.

Minder, Robert. "Die wiedergefundene Grossmutter: Bert Brechts schwäbische Herkunft." *Merkur,* 20 (1966), pp. 318–332.

Müller, Joachim. "Bertolt Brecht und sein lyrisches Lebenswerk." *Universitas,* 19 (1964), pp. 479–492.

Paul, Wolfgang. "Aus Brechts späten Jahren." *Neue deutsche Hefte,* 52 (1958), pp. 710–723.

SCHÖNE, ALBRECHT. "Bertolt Brecht: Theatertheorie und dramatische Dichtung." *Euphorion*, 52 (1958), pp. 272–296.

SÜSKIND, WILHELM EMANUEL. "Bert Brecht 1898–1956." *Die grossen Deutschen*, Volume V. Berlin: Propyläen-Verlag, 1957, pp. 510–518.

THIEME, KARL. "Des Teufels Gebetbuch? Eine Auseinandersetzung mit dem Werke Bertolt Brechts." *Hochland*, 29 (1932), pp. 394–413.

WALTER, HANS ALBERT. "Der Dichter der Dialektik." *Frankfurter Hefte*, 18 (1963), pp. 532–542.

5. Articles and Essays of a General Nature in English

ADLER, HENRY. "Bertolt Brecht's Theatre." *Twentieth Century* (August, 1956), pp. 114–134.

°BENTLEY, ERIC. Prefaces to the above-listed Brecht editions, as well as in some of his books, such as *In Search of Theater* (New York: A. Knopf, 1953); *The Life of the Drama* (New York: Athenaeum, 1965); *The Playwright as Thinker* (New York: Meridian Books, 1955.

BRUSTEIN, ROBERT. "Brecht against Brecht." *Partisan Review*, 30 (Spring, 1963), pp. 105–112.

CLURMAN, HAROLD. "The Achievement of Bertolt Brecht." *Partisan Review*, 26 (Fall, 1959), pp. 624–628.

ESSLIN, MARTIN. "Bert Brecht's Difficulties." *Encounter* (December, 1958), pp. 111–127.

————. "Brecht and the English Theatre." *Tulane Drama Review*, 11, 2 (Winter, 1966), pp. 63–70.

HELLER, PETER. "Nihilist into Activist: Two Phases in the Development of Bertolt Brecht." *Germanic Review*, 28 (1953), pp. 144–155.

HILL, CLAUDE. "Bertolt Brecht." *Symposium*, 15, 4 (Winter, 1961), pp. 245–270.

KERN, EDITH. "Brecht's Popular Theater and its American Popularity." *Modern Drama*, 3 (December, 1958), pp. 157–165.

SCHEVILL, JAMES. "Bertolt Brecht in New York." *Tulane Drama Review*, 6 (1961), pp. 98–107.

WEISSSTEIN, ULRICH. "From the Dramatic Novel to the Epic Theater: A Study of the Contemporary Background of Brecht's Theory and Practice." *Germanic Review*, 38 (1963), pp. 257–271.

————. "Brecht in America: a Preliminary Survey." *Modern Language Notes*, 4 (1963), pp. 373–396.

Index

207 *Index*